That Crazy English

Raps and Songs for Teaching English Literacy

Kathleen Leatherwood

That Crazy English Press ~ Reston

For information regarding permission, write to That Crazy English Press, 1621 Greenbriar Court, Reston, VA 20190

At the time of printing all publications, organizations, websites, and other resources exist as described in this book, and all have been verified as of October 2012. The author and That Crazy English Press make no warranty or guarantee regarding the information and materials given out by organizations or content found at websites, and we are not responsible for any changes that occur after this book's publication. Should you find an error or believe that a resource in this book is not as described, please contact That Crazy English Press. We strongly encourage parents, teachers, and other adults to monitor children's use of the Internet.

ISBN: 978-0-615-32906-2 (Spiral-bound Version)
ISBN: 978-0-9892380-0-7 (Paperback Version)
ISBN: 978-0-578-11874-1 (PDF Version)
ISBN: 978-0-9892380-1-4 (Audio CD)

Library of Congress Control Number: 2013949211

The Audio CD, PDF and Spiral-bound versions are available through the author's website www.ThatCrazyEnglish.com

Published by That Crazy English Press, Reston, VA

The author and publisher wish to thank those who have generously given permission to reprint borrowed material:

Images in the Reading Strategies Primary Bookmark © 2011 Rebecca Thinglev Grundahl, Albertslund, Denmark. Reprinted by permission of Rebecca Thinglev Grundahl and Tina Thinglev.

The Phono-Graphix® Paradigm © 1999, 2005 Read America, Inc.; reprinted by permission of Carmen and Geoffrey McGuinness.

Music created in PrintMusic by Finale®, Eden Prairie, MN
Cover piano vector image © iStockphoto.com/ Kalistratova
Cover design by Becky Anzalone
Author Photograph by Melanie Zucker Stanley

Table of Contents

I dedicate **That Crazy English** *to* ~

Carmen and Geoffrey McGuinness,
who got it first;

My students who led me down this musical path
so they could get it;

And my wonderful family and friends who
encouraged me to put it out there so that
everyone else could get it too.

That Crazy English
Introduction

From Speaking to Reading and Writing

All the raps/songs in *That Crazy English* were written as a direct response to the needs of English Language Learner (ELL) students and their native English-speaking peers. A familiar adage is, "If you can say it, you can write it." I like to go back one step and then take it to a logical conclusion: If you can think it, you can say it. If you can say it, you can write it. And if you can write it, others can read it and hear your voice as if they were right there with you. Writing is a written record of someone's ideas. It can last longer than that person's lifetime and be understood, or at least heard, by anyone able to read those words.

If you can think of an idea to express, you can say it, listen with your own ears, and write it down the way you want it to be read. I can use my eyes to *hear* your words any time I read them, even if I've never met you. The challenge with this process in English is that there are thousands of words to express our thoughts. Correctly using the ones we really want is not always so simple. The good news is that we can learn to manage the complexity if we crack the language code and embrace the many quirks of conventional English. To assist you on your literacy adventure, I have included a sample lesson plan for each type of rap/song.

Although many of these materials are presented as songs, the lyrics were composed first as raps. This may be more palatable to older students and adults. If read aloud as raps, I encourage you to introduce a steady beat by swaying or stepping in place, snapping fingers, tapping on the desk, or using a percussion instrument. This pulse beat emphasizes the rhythm and rhyme that are used as memory devices. I have found that students learn poems and songs quite readily and enthusiastically. Once learned, the songs prompt students to apply the content of the songs to their individual needs.

Speaking English

I begin with some basic grammar raps so that the conventions of spoken English become ingrained in our students' speech and thoughts for when they need to read and write them. The format is question and answer, and the seven raps cover present, past, and future tenses as well as the conditional mood. The raps incorporate the students' preferences and actions and begin in the present tense. They then expand into the other tenses and moods to use when students are ready to advance. It is not imperative to strictly follow the numbered sequence. Instead, choose the appropriate rap based on your students' needs to express themselves. These raps are appropriate for students in **grades pre-Kindergarten–adult**, with the understanding that pre-K students will be primarily learning them orally.

These raps are a jumping-off point to more complex sentences and discourse, but they contain the core of what is needed to express complete thoughts. Feel free to add descriptive phrases such as adjectives, names instead of pronouns, and adverbs for complexity once the basic pattern is understood. It is necessary for students to be able to both ask and answer questions so that they can transition easily from the raps to conversing with their peers and others. When these basic verb forms become automatic, students will be able to read them easily as well as begin to use them to express their own thoughts in writing. Please keep in mind that students will only begin to *write* correctly in English when they can *speak* correctly in English, so oral language development is critical to successful writing.

The Sounds of English

The Crazy English vowel songs (for **grades 2–adult**) were inspired by the work of Carmen and Geoffrey McGuinness, founders of Read America, Inc., and authors of *Reading Reflex*. Their method, Phono-Graphix, uses the nature of the English language itself, which began in the spoken form long before people started to write it down and read it. It is based on the *sounds* of the language, the letters that correspond to those sounds that make up words, and how to handle the variety and overlap in those sounds and letters. Not only is the nature of the language taken into account but also the nature of the child. Their paradigm, shown on the next page, was first developed and written down in 1993.

I wholeheartedly recommend using Phono-Graphix for teaching reading and writing, as it will systematically give your students the necessary framework to understand how English works. The Phono-Graphix method incorporates listening, speaking, reading, and writing in each of its lessons, using the nature of the student to discover the code while strengthening the skills necessary to read and write.

The Phono-Graphix® Paradigm

Letters are pictures of sounds

The nature of the code – these are pictures of sounds   b oa t

The nature of the child – *We believe that children can understand this perfectly well. Children have a remarkable ability to assess visual figures. At two days a baby can distinguish his mother's face from any other human face. Children assess and use visual figures in the world around them every day.*

Sometimes a sound picture is one letter and sometimes two or more

The nature of the code – the pictures can be made of one b / t or more oa letters

So boat has three sounds, and three sound pictures   b oa t

The nature of the child – *We believe children can manage this. They reuse figures in the world around them every day.*

■ square   ▲ triangle   🏠 house   *No rule was needed to recognize this as a house.*

So why would they need a rule to recognize   oa   as   'oe'.

There is variation in the code

The nature of the code – most of the sounds can be shown with more than one picture

b <u>oa</u> t   sl <u>ow</u>   m <u>o</u> s t   t <u>oe</u>   n <u>o</u> t e   th <u>ough</u>

The nature of the child – *We believe that children can easily learn that these*

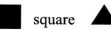   *are all pictures of the same sound. Children learn easily enough that*

these   *are pictures of the same word: flower.*

There is overlap in the code

The nature of the code – some of the pictures are used for more than one sound

<u>ow</u>   =   sh <u>ow</u>   f r <u>ow</u> n

The nature of the child – *We believe children can manage this as they easily manage that*

this ●   *can be a picture of a ball, a circle, a moon, a dot, **and more!***

The refrain of each vowel song contains the principle to apply when decoding or spelling the featured sound. I have focused on the vowels because of their confounding variety. I begin with the Basic Code: the twenty-two sound pictures that are the most straightforward. These sounds are usually found in some of the first words our students learn to speak, read, and write. Because they are the building blocks of many longer complex words, students must be secure in these initial sounds. With this knowledge, students can move from writing "cat" to "fantastic" with ease. In each vowel song the use of lowercase letters, when isolating just the vowel, denotes the *sound* of the vowels being presented. The use of capital letters denotes the *letter name*. It is crucial that students understand the difference between the letter name and the sound(s) the letters represent. Please note that the pronunciation in these songs is the General American or Standard American speech, reminiscent of the Midwestern accent used by many American broadcasters. There may still be some regional accents that could affect how your students spell.

Once students are ready to move on to the Advanced Code, they are ready to begin using the songs. The first vowel songs point out the difference between the Basic Code vowel and letter name without yet showing the variations. It will reinforce the sound they are learning and prepare them to *listen* for the advanced sounds. After reviewing the sounds of /a/, /o/, /i/, /u/, and /e/ through the songs (see lesson plan), they will be ready to learn that a sound can be represented by two or more letters. The book *Reading Reflex* will guide you through the recommended sequence for learning the Advanced Code.

These songs can easily be incorporated into a word study program such as *Words Their Way* or when teaching conventional spelling. The companion bookmarks are aids for students to use when reading, writing, or spelling words. Only the most commonly used variations are listed, so students may add to their bookmark as they find other spellings of the same sound. As students progress through the spelling continuum, they can exchange their current bookmark for the next level.

Reading English

The Reading Strategies raps/songs are based on strategies commonly used by strong readers in the classroom. The primary strategies are appropriate for students in **grades 1–3** as well as students of **any age** who are learning literacy skills. Graphics are included on the bookmarks to enhance memory.

The intermediate strategies are appropriate for **grades 3–adult.** The graphics have been intentionally omitted for students to personalize their bookmarks with their own graphics, showing their understanding of each of the eight strategies as they are discussed. As a bonus, the instructor can discern what strategies have been covered instructionally with a quick glance at the bookmark. The strategies can be covered in the teacher's preferred sequence, and the students' bookmarks will alert the teacher to those who may have been absent for a strategy lesson. Students use the bookmarks while they read to serve as a reminder of the reading strategies as they seek to understand the text.

"The Parts of a Story" describes the vocabulary of fiction writing (character, setting, problem, solution) and uses a refrain of question words that guide readers to understand what the author has written. Readers can then incorporate these features in their own fiction writing. A set of word cards is included for practice in retelling a story or writing.

Writing English

The Writing Strategies songs cover the writing form of a one to five paragraph essay, as well as revising and editing tips. They are appropriate for use by students in **grades 4–adult.** The songs incorporate many of the principles of the Writing Workshop, encouraging students to

- plan their writing
- use an introduction, body, and conclusion
- choose words that are precise
- use complex sentences
- use standard English and American spelling
- use correct punctuation and capitalization
- incorporate standard English grammar and usage

It is my hope that the habit of rereading *aloud* during and after writing becomes a joy rather than the chore most students find it to be. An important point to make to students about the writing songs is that the "reader" referred to in each song is not just the teacher or a peer. Rather, the most important reader is the student writer who strives to present the best work possible through his or her own written voice.

This material is formatted in three ways: music notation to provide the melody and chords for musical accompaniment; lyric sheets, which can be used as raps or song sheets for students; and a chord sheet for ease in using a piano, guitar, or autoharp while singing along. I purposefully did not add visuals to the lyric sheets in the vowel songs, as I hope the students will illustrate the model words themselves to make them more meaningful and personal.

The songs in *That Crazy English* can be used in various ways while teaching the content material and serve as enhancements to a balanced language arts curriculum. The grammar raps can be used as warm-ups or during circle time in the lower grades. The vowel songs can be used to introduce the target vowel sound and then be revisited during practice and culminating activities. Your students may be inspired, and should be encouraged, to compose their own verses once they understand the target features. For the reading and writing rap/songs, I suggest introducing the relevant verses after the content has been taught to the students, leaving the entire song until all the features have been covered.

The songs and bookmarks are designed as gentle reminders of what the student has learned, which I hope will move from a mental checklist to an unconscious behavior in the process of reading and writing. Enjoy singing or rapping your way through the English language!

Kathleen Leatherwood
October 2012

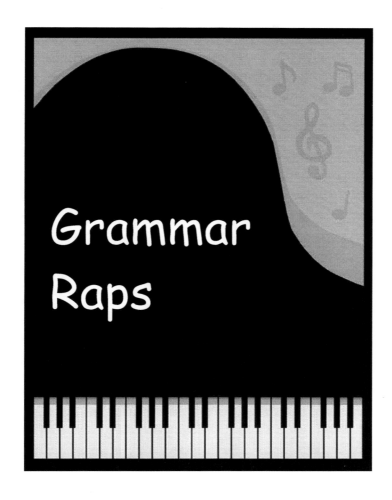

Grammar Raps

Do You Like It?
Are You Smiling?
Did You Do It?
Were You Smiling?
Have You Ever?
Will You Do It?
Would You Like It?
Uh-oh!

Grammar Raps Guide

I am grateful to Carolyn Graham for opening my eyes and ears to Jazz Chants at the Teachers of English for Speakers of Other Languages (TESOL) convention in Baltimore, Maryland, in 2003. In her inimitable manner, she had us all tapping, clapping, and chanting away with great abandon. My own raps are a result of noticing the needs of my students in their daily conversations and creating a structure in which they could practice. Two of my goals were to ingrain in my students the elusive third person "s" and the past tense using "did" through repetition, relevance, and the rhythm of spoken English. Although the repetition may seem tedious and unnecessary to a native English speaker, it brings comfort and confidence to those new to English sounds and conventions.

The raps are meant to be informal, enjoyable, and based on the interests of your students. Have fun trying out a variety of voices and interpretations to enhance meaning in both the question and answer parts. Personalize the raps by using vocal expression and adding details, as shown in the example below:

Were you *reading*?	*Stress action*
Yes, I was.	*Normal response*
Were *you* reading?	*Stress person*
Yes, *I* was.	*Slightly annoyed*
Were you *really* reading?	*Add a little doubt*
Yes, I *was*.	*Insistent*
I was reading my novel late last night.	*Object and time added*

Or

Did you do it?	*Whisper*
Yes, I did.	*Mimic whisper or respond normally*
Did you do it?	*Normal voice*
Yes, I did.	*Normal voice*
Did you do it?	*Louder, demanding voice*
Yes, I did.	*Insistent*
I did my homework an hour ago.	*Object and time added*

The rap flows from everyday conversation to more complex sentence structures used in conventional writing; hence, with practice, students can eventually move from a simple rap line, "I was reading," to a descriptive sentence, "Late last night as I was reading my novel, I heard a loud crash downstairs in the kitchen." Each student will be challenged at his or her own level, and the feedback you receive will inform the next steps in your instruction.

The raps can be used in any way you wish using two groups of speakers. The teacher introduces the topic and vocabulary, and the students practice the sounds and ask for any clarification necessary. In the beginning, the teacher poses the question, and a student or the entire class responds, guided by the teacher. Once the students are comfortable with the format and the rap's vocabulary, the whole group can ask the question to an individual or any other combination of speakers that works with your class. As a more physical activity, the room can be divided into YES and NO areas to which the class members can move according to their personal preferences. For example, the teacher may ask, "Do you like to swim?" and the students then move to their choice of areas. They can then take turns responding individually, "Yes, I do; I like to swim" or "No, I don't; I don't like to swim." You could end with each group asking the other and answering appropriately, "Yes, we do; we like to swim" or "No, we don't; we don't like to swim." The teacher could follow up by asking, "Do they like to swim?" or "Does Maria like to swim?" and the whole class would look to find the answer and respond appropriately. The possibilities are numerous!

It is also beneficial to pair up students to practice asking and answering questions in a conversational format without the repetition of the rap. This is a nice bridge for students to use on their way to expanding into independently writing conventional sentences. Please refer to the grammar raps lesson on the next page to help you get started.

Grammar Raps Lesson

Materials

- Chart paper, chalkboard, white board, or SMART Board
- Copy of "Do You Like It?" in a large format
- Pointer
- Hat, bag, or box for selecting cards
- Magazines for cutting out additional pictures of activities
- Word and picture cards of activities for sorting such as:

swim	sing	run	knit	sew	ski
surf	bike	walk	play games	play cards	travel

Introduction (5 minutes)

Show students one of the activity pictures, such as "swim," and ask, "What does this person like to do?" Write the activity word on the board. Ask the students, "Do you like to swim?" The students will probably answer "Yes" or "No." Model the full answers: "Yes, I do" and "No, I don't." Ask the students what other activities they like to do and write those words on the board, having the students fill in one of the blank cards for each activity. If students don't know the word they want to add, have them act out the action and then you can write the word on the board.

Large Group Lesson (10 minutes)

Place the word and picture cards into the hat. Select one student to choose a card from the hat and tell the class that they will be asking that person if she or he likes to do that activity. Direct the other students to ask the question along with you, looking at the person, "Do you like to _____?" If the student just answers "Yes" or "No," supply the entire answer: "Yes, I do" or "No, I don't." Offer the hat to another student and continue having the class ask the question, "Do you like to _____?" with the student answering with the complete rejoinder. After you have done 6–8 words, show the students the large-format rap "Do You Like It?" Divide the class into two groups, one group to ask the question and the other to answer it. Using the pointer, have students practice the rap, using both the positive and negative responses. Alternate the groups so that they each get a chance to ask and answer the questions. Emphasize the use of the complete answer: "I like to _____, yes, indeed" or "I don't like to _____, no sirree."

Small Group Practice (10 minutes)

Give students the magazines to search for activities to cut out. Alternatively, students may draw an activity if they don't find one that they like. They should say the word aloud and then write it on a blank card. After each student has found two activities, have the class practice asking each other questions using the rap format, including the repetition and complete answer at the end.

Large Group Summary (5 minutes)

Gather students together again and designate a place in the room for "Yes" answers and one for "No" answers. Select a student to ask a question and direct students to move to the appropriate place. Once there, the whole group can answer using the rap format, with the volunteer asking the question and the group answering as individuals. Start with the "Yes" group and then repeat the rap with the "No" group.

What's Next (5 minutes)

Tell students they will be expanding the rap to include objects they like as well as activities. Ask them to make a list of what they like and to bring one object to the next class. When students are ready, expand the questions to "Does he like _____?" ("Yes he does; he likes _____."), "Do they like _____?" and so on until all verb forms are used. Also, as a quick warm-up at the beginning of a lesson, students can act out an activity for the class to guess and then ask the class if they like to do that activity, using the rap format.

Do You Like It?
Present Tense (1)

Do you like it?
   Yes, I do.
Do you like it?
   Yes, I do.
Do you like it?
   Yes, I do.
I like it, yes indeed.

Do you like pizza?
   Yes I do.
Do you like pizza?
   Yes, I do.
Do you like pizza?
   Yes I do.
I like pizza, yes indeed.

Do you like to swim?
   Yes, I do.
Do you like to swim?
   Yes, I do.
Do you like to swim?
   Yes, I do.
I like to swim, yes indeed.

Do you like it?
   No, I don't.
Do you like it?
   No, I don't.
Do you like it?
   No, I don't.
I don't like it, no sirree.

Do you like soccer?
   No, I don't.
Do you like soccer?
   No, I don't.
Do you like soccer?
   No, I don't.
I don't like soccer, no sirree.

Do you like to sit?
   No, I don't.
Do you like to sit?
   No, I don't.
Do you like to sit?
   No, I don't.
I don't like to sit, no sirree.

Variations:

Does he like _____?
   Yes, he does. etc.
He **likes**... etc.

Do they like to _____?
   Yes, they do. etc.

Does she like _____?
   No, she doesn't. etc.
   She doesn't like... etc.

Do you all like to _____?
   No, we don't. etc.

Are You Smiling?
Present Progressive Tense (2)

Are you smiling?
  Yes, I am.
Are you smiling?
  Yes, I am.
Are you smiling?
  Yes, I am.
I am smiling, yes indeed.
(I'm smiling now, yes indeed.)

Is he thinking?
  Yes, he is.
Is he thinking?
  Yes, he is.
Is he thinking?
  Yes, he is.
He is thinking, yes indeed.
(He's thinking now, yes indeed.)

Are they talking?
  Yes they are.
Are they talking?
  Yes they are.
Are they talking?
  Yes they are.
They are talking, yes indeed.
(They're talking now, yes indeed.

Are you laughing?
  No, I'm not.
Are you laughing?
  No, I'm not.
Are you laughing?
  No, I'm not.
I'm not laughing, no sirree.
(I am not laughing, no sirree.)

Is she texting?
  No, she isn't. (No, she's not.)
Is she texting?
  No, she isn't. (No, she's not.)
Is she texting?
  No, she isn't. (No, she's not.)
She isn't texting, no sirree.
(She is not texting, no sirree.)
(She's not texting, no sirree.)

Are you all sleeping?
  No, we aren't. (No, we're not.)
Are you all sleeping?
  No, we aren't. (No, we're not.)
Are you all sleeping?
  No, we aren't. (No, we're not.)
We aren't sleeping, no sirree.
(We are not sleeping, no sirree.)
(We're not sleeping, no sirree.)

NOTE: The -ing verbs (gerunds) may also be replaced by adjectives for simple speaking practice, and can be paired with opposites: **Are you happy? Is he sad? etc.**

Did You Do It?
Past Tense (3)

Did you do it?
   Yes, I did.
Did you do it?
   Yes, I did.
Did you do it?
   Yes, I did.
I did it, yes indeed.

Did you like it?
   Yes, I did.
Did you like it?
   Yes, I did.
Did you like it?
   Yes, I did.
I **did** like it, yes indeed.
(I **liked** it, yes indeed.)

Variations:

Did he get it?
   Yes, he did. etc.
He **did** get it, yes indeed.
(He **got** it, yes indeed.)

Did they see it?
   Yes, they did. etc.
They **did** see it, yes indeed.
(They **saw** it, yes indeed.)

Did you do it?
   No, I didn't.
Did you do it?
   No, I didn't.
Did you do it?
   No, I didn't.
I didn't do it, no sirree.

Did you finish it?
   No, I didn't.
Did you finish it?
   No, I didn't.
Did you finish it?
   No, I didn't.
I **didn't** finish it, no sirree.
(I never **finished** it, no
   sirree.)

Did she get it?
   No, she didn't. etc.
She **didn't** get it, no sirree.
(She never **got** it, no sirree.)

Did you all see it?
   No, we didn't. etc.
We **didn't** see it, no sirree.
(We never **saw** it, no sirree.)

Bold words show that there is only **one** past tense form in the verbal phrase when **did** is used ("**did** see" versus "**did saw**").

Were You Smiling?
Past Progressive Tense (4)

Were you smiling?
    Yes, I was.
Were you smiling?
    Yes, I was.
Were you smiling?
    Yes, I was.
I was smiling, yes indeed.

Was he singing?
    Yes, he was.
Was he singing?
    Yes, he was.
Was he singing?
    Yes, he was.
He was singing, yes indeed

Were they eating?
    Yes, they were.
Were they eating?
    Yes, they were.
Were they eating?
    Yes, they were.
They were eating, yes indeed.

Were you laughing?
    No, I wasn't.
Were you laughing?
    No, I wasn't.
Were you laughing?
    No, I wasn't.
I wasn't laughing, no sirree.
(I was *not* laughing, no sirree.)

Was she dancing?
    No, she wasn't.
Was she dancing?
    No, she wasn't.
Was she dancing?
    No, she wasn't.
She wasn't dancing, no sirree.
(She was *not* dancing, no sirree.)

Were you all reading?
    No, we weren't.
Were you all reading?
    No, we weren't.
Were you all reading?
    No, we weren't.
We weren't reading, no sirree.
(We were *not* reading, no sirree.)

NOTE: The -ing verbs (gerunds) may also be replaced by adjectives for simple speaking practice and can be paired with opposites: Were you happy? Was he sad? etc.

Have You Ever?
Present Perfect Tense (5)

Have you ever traveled?
   Yes, I have.
Have you ever traveled?
   Yes, I have.
Have you ever traveled?
   Yes, I have.
I have traveled, yes indeed.
(I've traveled before, yes indeed.)

Has he ever run?
   Yes, he has.
Has he ever run?
   Yes, he has.
Has he ever run?
   Yes, he has.
He has run, yes indeed.
(He's run fast, yes indeed.)

Have they ever giggled?
   Yes, they have.
Have they ever giggled?
   Yes, they have.
Have they ever giggled?
   Yes, they have.
They have giggled, yes indeed.
(They've giggled a lot, yes indeed.)

Have you ever skated?
   No, I haven't.
Have you ever skated?
   No, I haven't.
Have you ever skated?
   No, I haven't.
I haven't skated, no sirree.
(I've never skated, no sirree.)

Has she ever driven?
   No, she hasn't.
Has she ever driven?
   No, she hasn't.
Has she ever driven?
   No, she hasn't.
She hasn't driven, no sirree.
(She's never driven, no sirree.)

Have you all ever frowned?
   No, we haven't.
Have you all ever frowned?
   No, we haven't.
Have you all ever frowned?
   No, we haven't.
We haven't frowned, no sirree.
(We've never frowned, no
   siree.)

Will You Do It?
Future Tense (6)

Will you do it?
   Yes, I will.
Will you do it?
   Yes, I will.
Will you do it?
   Yes, I will.
I will do it, yes indeed.
(I'll do it, yes indeed.)

Will you buy it?
   Yes, I will.
Will you buy it?
   Yes, I will.
Will you buy it?
   Yes, I will.
I will buy it, yes indeed.
(I'll buy it today, yes indeed.)

Variations:

Will he get it?
   Yes, he will. etc.
He *will* get it, yes indeed.
He will *get* it today, yes indeed.
(He'll get it today, yes indeed.)

Will they see it?
   Yes, they will. etc.
They will see it, yes indeed.
(They'll see it today, yes indeed.)

Will you do it?
   No, I won't.
Will you do it?
   No, I won't.
Will you do it?
   No, I won't.
I won't do it, no sirree.
(I will not do it, no sirree.)
(I'll never do it, no sirree.)

Will you sell it?
   No, I won't.
Will you sell it?
   No, I won't.
Will you sell it?
   No, I won't.
I won't sell it, no sirree.
(I'll never sell it, no sirree.)

Will she get it?
   No, she won't. etc.
She won't get it, no sirree.
(She will *never* get it, no sirree.)
(She'll never *get* it, no sirree.)

Will you all see it?
   No, we won't. etc.
We won't see it, no sirree.
(We'll never see it, no sirree.)

Would You Like It?
Conditional Mood (7)

Would you like it?
   Yes, I would.
Would you like it?
   Yes, I would.
Would you like it?
   Yes, I would.
I would like it, yes indeed.
(I'd like it, yes indeed)

Would she like pizza?
   Yes she would.
Would she like pizza?
   Yes she would.
Would she like pizza?
   Yes she would.
She would like pizza, yes indeed.
(She'd like pizza, yes indeed.)

Would they like to play?
   Yes, they would.
Would they like to play?
   Yes, they would.
Would they like to play?
   Yes, they would.
They would like to play, yes indeed.
(They'd like to play, yes indeed.)

Would you keep it?
   No, I wouldn't.
Would you keep it?
   No, I wouldn't.
Would you keep it?
   No, I wouldn't.
I wouldn't keep it, no sirree.
(I would not keep it, no sirree.)

Would he like coffee?
   No, he wouldn't.
Would he like coffee?
   No, he wouldn't
Would he like coffee?
   No, he wouldn't.
He wouldn't like coffee, no sirree.
(He would *not* like coffee, no
   sirree)

Would you all like to eat?
   No, we wouldn't.
Would you all like to eat?
   No, we wouldn't.
Would you all like to eat?
   No, we wouldn't.
We wouldn't like to eat, no sirree.
(We would *not* like to eat, no
   sirree.)

Uh-oh!
Common slang words used in dialogue

	Person 1	Person 2	
Hey, you! (quietly)	Psst!		
		Huh? Whadja say?	What? What did you say?
Be quiet, Hush	Shh!		
		Unh-uh	No. Also, Nuh-*uh*
Thoughtful, Thinking	Hmm...		
		No way.	Definitely not
Tsk: Disgust, Disdain	Tsk, look!		
		Meh – uh-oh!	Meh: I don't care, Whatever
Uh-huh: Yes	Uh-huh, You see?		Uh-oh: Oh dear
		Mm-hm. I know.	Mm-hm: Yes
ZZZZ: Sound of snoring	Someone's sleeping. ZZZZ...		
		Ahem, *yeah, Shh!*	Ahem: Throat clearing to get someone's attention
	Shh!		
	Shh!	Shh!	

18

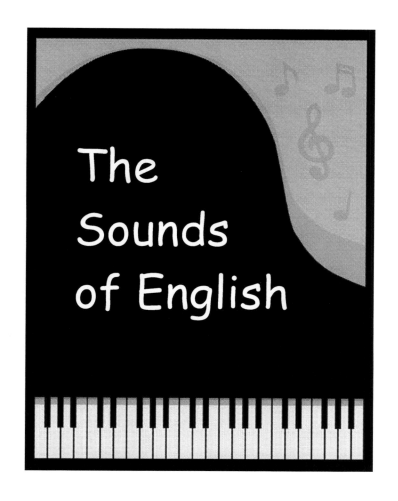

The
Sounds
of English

Letters represent sounds: a, o, i, u, e

One sound, 2 or more letters: th, sh, ch

Sound the same, look different: ow, ou,
   A, O, I, U, E, er, oy, aw

Look the same, sound different: OW,
   OO, OUGH

That Crazy English Guide

These raps/songs have been written to assist the memory in dealing with the variety of English vowels. Using pictures to illustrate the words in the songs will add another way to jog the memory. The lyric sheets have been designed so that there is plenty of space for students to draw their own pictures of the words in the lyrics. Some students may prefer to draw one picture to remind them of the featured sound, and others may want to add their own words. As long as the sound is the same as the one featured in the song, students should draw what works best for their particular learning style.

As an instructor, you will decide how to use the materials in this book, based on your experience and word study or spelling curriculum requirements. Below are suggestions to guide you, and there are additional references at the end of the book to also help your lesson planning. A specific lesson plan is also included following these general guidelines.

Suggested Lesson Procedure

- **Large Group Lesson.** Use realia (actual objects) or pictures to introduce the featured sound to the whole class or word study group. Solicit more words from students to ensure they are hearing the sound correctly. Sort a number of words together in the whole group to check for understanding of how to sort the sounds. Introduce the song to students using a large format of the lyrics on chart paper, overhead, SMART Board, et cetera. Introduce the set of pictures and words for this feature.

- **Small Group Practice.** Provide sets of words and pictures for sorting and let students work in pairs to practice sorting the featured sound. Circulate among students to ensure they know what the pictures and words are and that they are sorting them correctly.

- **Large Group Summary.** Return to the large group to share what students have discovered in their sorting and to clarify any misunderstandings.

- **What's Next?** Provide Post-it notes for students to find their own similar words as they read during the next few days. They could then post them on a chart in the classroom. Give each student a lyric sheet to illustrate the featured words and to help them remember the sound. These can be kept in a word study notebook to refer to throughout the year.

- Establish how you want to assess students' understanding, such as a spelling test or sorting activity. Encourage students to make up their own verses to the songs to show their understanding of that particular feature.

- Decide how you want to introduce the bookmarks. They are grouped based on the Phono-Graphix principles and suggested vowel sequence and would be most useful after an entire principle has been studied. The bookmarks are easy references for students to have nearby when reading or writing.

That Crazy English Lesson *a*

Materials

- Chart paper, chalkboard, white board, or SMART Board
- Copy of "That Crazy English *a*" in a large format
- Pointer
- Assorted realia or photos of various objects having an /a/ sound
- A hat, bag, or box for selecting cards
- Word and picture cards for sorting such as:

cat	sat	sand	hand	hat	rake
fan	pan	mask	ant	can	table
cake	mail	rain	nail	plane	sail

Introduction (5 minutes)
Show students an apple and ask them what it is. Have students repeat the first sound /a/. Show students a cat (picture, plush toy, etc) and ask what it is. Have students break the three sounds apart (c-a-t) and emphasize the /a/ sound. Ask students what other words they know that use the /a/ sound. Write those words that have the /a/ sound on the board.

Large Group Lesson (10 minutes)
Ask students, "What do we write when we want the /a/ sound?" Write /a/ on the board. If students use the letter name, tell them that "A" is the *name* of that letter, but it has other sounds, such as the /a/ in cat. Have a hat and some items or cards with pictures of objects that have and don't have the /a/ sound. As students choose from the hat, they say the name of the object and sort it into two lists of /a/ and not /a/. After the students have sorted 6–8 words for /a/ and not/a/, sing verse 1 and the chorus of "That Crazy English *a*," using the pointer to remind students that sometimes the letter A will sound like /a/ or like A. Tell students that the /a/ sound is the one that is used more, so it will be their first choice when they read or write a word.

Small Group Practice (10 minutes)
Give students their own sheets of /a/ and non/a/ pictures and matching words to cut out and sort in pairs. They should say the words aloud and then decide where to place the words or pictures. As students are sorting, make sure they are saying the words correctly and supply the words if they don't recognize or know them. At this point, don't use any alternate sounds for A, such as **ball** or **walk**. See the note below under What's Next?

Large Group Summary (5 minutes)
Gather students together again and ask them what they noticed about the pictures and words. They will probably say that when they said the words aloud, some had an A sound, others had an /a/ sound, and some words had other vowels along with an A.

What's Next? (5 minutes)
Tell students that they will be listening for the /a/ sound for the next few days and that they are to write any words they find on sticky notes to bring to the next few word study sessions. Students may find other sounds for the letter A as well. They should bring those words to the next session, and you can then add the second verse, which gives a variety of the sounds of the letter A. At this point, you can sort these new words under "not /a/" to ensure that students hear the /a/ sound consistently. Once the song is introduced, students should be given the lyric sheets for their word study notebooks and can then add their own illustrations for the words in the lyrics or words they personally like that use the same vowel sound.

That Crazy English Intro/Tag

Kathleen Leatherwood

Note: When reading the individual letter sounds,
lowercase letters denote the *sound* as in the example word, and
UPPERCASE letters denote the *letter name* as in the alphabet.

A B C D E F G___ It seems as ea-sy as can be.

Ev-'ry let-ter has a name But in Eng-lish they don't al - ways

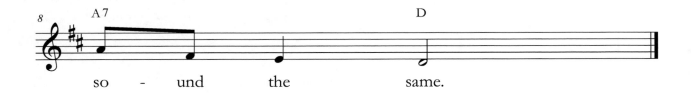

so - und the same.

This introduction can be sung at the beginning or end
of any of the Crazy English vowel raps/songs.

That Crazy English *a*

Kathleen Leatherwood

Note: When reading the individual letter sounds,
lowercase letters denote the *sound* as in the example word, and
UPPERCASE letters denote the *letter name* as in the alphabet.

a a a is the sound in cat__ In ap - ple, fan, and
words like that But if cake is what you want to write You've
got to have an A to ma-ke it right. a a a is the
sound in cat But it does-n't al-ways sound that way. A A A is the
let-ter name but it does-n't al-ways so-und the same.

2. Tall, ball, fall, and that's not all
Talk and walk, and even small
Saw and was and cat don't rhyme
But you use the letter A every time.

Refrain

© 2009 Kathleen Leatherwood

23

That Crazy English *a*
Lyrics

Note: When reading the individual letter sounds,
lowercase letters denote the *sound* as in the example word, and
UPPERCASE letters denote the *letter name* as in the alphabet.

Verses:

a   a   a   is the sound in **cat**

In **apple**, **fan**, and words like **that**

But if **cake** is what you want to write

You've got to have an **A** to make it right.

Tall, **ball**, **fall**, and that's not **all**

Talk and **walk** and even **small**

Saw and **was** and **cat** don't rhyme

But you use the letter **A** every time.

Refrain:

a   a   a   is the sound in **cat**

But it doesn't always sound that way.

A   A   A   is the letter name

But it doesn't always **sound** the same.

That Crazy English *a*
Chords

Note: When reading the individual letter sounds,
lowercase letters denote the *sound* as in the example word, and
UPPERCASE letters denote the *letter name* as in the alphabet.

Verse 1:

D   A7
a   a   a is the sound in **cat**

     A7   D
In **apple**, **fan**, and words like **that**

       G   D
But if **cake** is what you want to write

     A7   A7
You've got to have an **A** to make it

  D
right.

Refrain:

G   D
a   a   a   is the sound in **cat**

     A7   D
But it doesn't always **sound** that
way.

G   D
A A A is the letter name

     A7   A7   A7
But it doesn't always **sound**

    D
the same.

Verse 2:

D   A7
Tall, **ball**, **fall**, and that's not **all**

A7   D
Talk and **walk** and even **small**

G   D
Saw and **was** and **cat** don't rhyme

     A7   A7   D
But you use the letter **A** every time.

25

That Crazy English *o*

Kathleen Leatherwood

Note: When reading the individual letter sounds,
lowercase letters denote the *sound* as in the example word, and
UPPERCASE letters denote the *letter name* as in the alphabet.

2. Octopus and mom and drop
    Box and got, and even shop.
    Stone and or and hot don't rhyme,
    But they use the letter O every time.

    Refrain

That Crazy English *o*
Lyrics

Note: When reading the individual letter sounds,
lowercase letters denote the *sound* as in the example word, and
UPPERCASE letters denote the *letter name* as in the alphabet.

Verses:

o   o   o   is the sound in **hot**

In **hop** and **dog**, and even **pot**

But if **hope** is what you want to write

You've got to have an **O** to make it right.

Octopus, and **mom** and **drop**

Box and **got** and even **shop**

Stone and **or** and **hot** don't rhyme

But you use the letter **O** every time.

Refrain:

   o   o   o   is the sound in **hot**

   But it doesn't always **sound** that way.

   O   O   O   is the letter name

   But it doesn't always **sound** the same.

That Crazy English *o*
Chords

Note: When reading the individual letter sounds,
lowercase letters denote the *sound* as in the example word, and
UPPERCASE letters denote the *letter name* as in the alphabet.

Verse 1:

D   A7
o   o   o   is the sound in **hot**

     A7   D
In **hop** and **dog**, and even **pot**

       G   D
But if **hope** is what you want to
write

      A7   A7
You've got to have an **O** to make it

  D
right.

Refrain:

G   D
o   o   o   is the sound in **hot**

    A7   D
But it doesn't always sound that
way.

G   D
O   O   O   is the letter name

    A7   A7   A7
But it doesn't always **sound**

D
the same.

Verse 2:

D   A7
Octopus, and **mom** and **drop**

A7   D
Box and **got** and even **shop**

G   D
Stone and **or** and **hot** don't rhyme

      A7   A7   D
But you use the letter **O** every time.

That Crazy English *i*

Kathleen Leatherwood

Note: When reading the individual letter sounds,
lowercase letters denote the *sound* as in the example word, and
UPPERCASE letters denote the *letter name* as in the alphabet.

2.   Iglooo, his, and fill and fit
Twig and tip, and even hit.
Bike and girl and pig don't rhyme,
But you use the letter I every time.

Refrain

29

That Crazy English *i*
Lyrics

Note: When reading the individual letter sounds,
lowercase letters denote the *sound* as in the example word, and
UPPERCASE letters denote the *letter name* as in the alphabet.

Verses:

i i i   is the sound in **big**

In **win** and **did**, and even **pig**

But if **time** is what you want to write

You've got to have an **I** to make it right.

Igloo, **his**, and **fill** and **fit**

Twig and **tip** and even **hit**

Bike and **girl** and **pig** don't rhyme

But you use the letter **I** every time.

Refrain:

i i i   is the sound in **big**

But it doesn't always **sound** that way.

I I I   is the letter name

But it doesn't always **sound** the same.

That Crazy English *i*
Chords

Note: When reading the individual letter sounds,
   lowercase letters denote the *sound* as in the example word, and
   UPPERCASE letters denote the *letter name* as in the alphabet.

Verse 1:

D   A7
i   i   i   is the sound in **big**

   A7   D
In **win** and **did**, and even **pig**

        G   D
But if **time** is what you want to write

       A7   A7
You've got to have an **I** to make it

  D
right.

Verse 2:

D   A7
Igloo, **his**, and **fill** and **fit**

A7   D
Twig and **tip,** and even **hit**

G   D
Bike and **girl** and **pig** don't rhyme

       A7   A7   D
But you use the letter **I** every time.

Refrain:

G   D
i   i   i   is the sound in **big**

      A7   D
But it doesn't always **sound** that
way.

G   D
I   **I**   **I** is the letter name

       A7   A7   A7
But it doesn't always **sound**

    D
the same.

That Crazy English *u*

Kathleen Leatherwood

Note: When reading the individual letter sounds,
lowercase letters denote the *sound* as in the example word, and
UPPERCASE letters denote the *letter name* as in the alphabet.

2.   Umbrella and rug and tug
     Fun and run, and even slug
     Burger and bun and you don't rhyme,
     But you use the letter U every time.

     Refrain

That Crazy English *u*
Lyrics

Note: When reading the individual letter sounds,
lowercase letters denote the *sound* as in the example word, and
UPPERCASE letters denote the *letter name* as in the alphabet.

Verses:

u   u   u   is the sound in **up**

In **sun** and **nut**, and even **pup**

But if **blue** is what you want to write

You've got to have a **U** to make it right.

Umbrella and **rug** and **tug**

Fun and **run** and even **slug**

Burger and **bun** and **you** don't rhyme

But you use the letter **U** every time.

Refrain:

u   u   u   is the sound in **up**

But it doesn't always **sound** that way.

U **U** **U** is the letter name,

But it doesn't always **sound** the same.

That Crazy English *u*
Chords

Verse 1:

D   A7
u   u   u is the sound in **up**

     A7   D
In **sun** and **nut**, and even **pup**

        G   D
But if **blue** is what you want to write

       A7
You've got to have a **U** to make it

  D
right.

Refrain:

G   D
u   u   u is the sound in **up**

       A7   D
But it doesn't always **sound** that way.

G   D
U   U   U is the letter name

       A7   A7   A7
But it doesn't always **sound**

    D
the same.

Verse 2:

D   A7
Umbrella and **rug** and **tug**

A7   D
Fun and **bun**, and even **slug**

G   D
Burger and **bun** and **you** don't rhyme

G   D
But you use the letter **U** every time.

That Crazy English *e*

Kathleen Leatherwood

Note: When reading the individual letter sounds,
lowercase letters denote the *sound* as in the example word, and
UPPERCASE letters denote the *letter name* as in the alphabet.

2. Elephant and bed and Ben
    Met and let, and even ten
    Fed and street and the don't rhyme
    But you use the letter E every time.

Refrain

That Crazy English *e*
Lyrics

Note: When reading the individual letter sounds,
lowercase letters denote the *sound* as in the example word, and
UPPERCASE letters denote the *letter name* as in the alphabet.

Verses:

e   e   e   is the sound in **pet**

In **hen** and **leg**, and even **net**

But if **sweet** is what you want to write

You've got to have an **E** to make it right.

Elephant and **bed** and **Ben**

Met and **let** and even **ten**

Fed and **street** and **the** don't rhyme

But you use the letter **E** every time.

Refrain:

e   e   e   is the sound in **pet**

But it doesn't always **sound** that way.

E   E   E   is the letter name

But it doesn't always **sound** the same.

That Crazy English *e*
Chords

Verse 1:

D   A7
e e e is the sound in **pet**

  A7   D
In **hen** and **leg** and even **net**

     G   D
But if **sweet** is what you want to write

    A7   A7
You've got to have an **E** to make it

  D
right.

Verse 2:

D   A7
Elephant and **bed** and **Ben**

A7   D
Met and **let** and even **ten**

G   D
Fed and **street** and **the** don't rhyme

      A7   A7 D
But you use the letter **E** every time.

Refrain:

G   D
e e e is the sound in **pet**

    A7   D
But it doesn't always **sound** that way.

G   D
E E E is the letter name

    A7   A7   A7
But it doesn't always **sound**

    D
the same.

That Crazy English
First Vowels
Lyrics

Note: **When reading the individual letter sounds,
lowercase letters denote the *sound* as in the example word, and
UPPERCASE letters denote the *letter name* as in the alphabet.**

A B C D E F G
It seems as easy as can be.
Every letter has a name
But in English they don't always
   sound the same.

Verse 1:
a a a is the sound in **cat**
In **apple**, **fan**, and words like **that**
But if **cake** is what you want to write
You've got to have an **A** to make it right.

Tall, **ball**, **fall**, and that's not **all**
Talk and **walk**, and even **small**
Saw and **was** and **cat** don't rhyme
But you use the letter **A** every time.

Refrain:
a a a is the sound in **cat**
But it doesn't always sound that way.
A A A is the letter name
But it doesn't always **sound** the same.

Verse 2:
e e e is the sound in **pet**
In **hen** and **leg**, and words like **net**
But if **sweet** is what you want to write
You've got to have an **E** to make it right.

Elephant and **bed** and **Ben**
Met and **let**, and even **ten**
Fed and **street** and **the** don't rhyme
But you use the letter **E** every time.

Refrain:
e e e is the sound in **pet**
But it doesn't always **sound** that way.
E E E is the letter name
But it doesn't always **sound** the same.

Verse 3:
i i i is the sound in **big**
In **win** and **did**, and even **pig**
But if **time** is what you want to write
You've got to have an **I** to make it right.

Igloo, **his**, and **fill** and **fit**
Twig and **tip**, and even **hit**
Bike and **girl** and **pig** don't rhyme
But you use the letter **I** every time.

Refrain:
i i i is the sound in **big**
But it doesn't always sound that way.
I I I is the letter name,
But it doesn't always **sound** the same.

That Crazy English
First Vowels
Lyrics

Note: **When reading the individual letter sounds,
lowercase letters denote the *sound* as in the example word, and
UPPERCASE letters denote the *letter name* as in the alphabet.**

Verse 4:

o   o   o   is the sound in **hot**
In **hop** and **dog**, and even **pot**
But if **hope** is what you want to write
You've got to have an **O** to make it right.

Octopus, and **mom** and **drop**
Box and **got**, and even **shop**
Stone and **or** and **hot** don't rhyme
But you use the letter **O** every time.

Refrain:

o   o   o   is the sound in **hot**
But it doesn't always sound that way.
O   O   O is the letter name
But it doesn't always **sound** the same.

Verse 5:

u   u   u   is the sound in **up**
In **sun** and **nut**, and even **pup**
Burger and **bun** and **you** don't rhyme
But you use the letter **U** every time.

Refrain:

u   u   u   is the sound in **up**
But it doesn't always sound that way.
U   U   U is the letter name
But it doesn't always **sound** the same.

Bookmark 1

e
e pet

u
u up

i
i big

o
o hot

a
a cat

That Crazy English Bookmark 1
© 2011 Kathleen Leatherwood

Bookmark 2

e
e pet

u
u up

i
i big

o
o hot

a
a cat

That Crazy English Bookmark 1
© 2011 Kathleen Leatherwood

Bookmark 3

e
e pet

u
u up

i
i big

o
o hot

a
a cat

That Crazy English Bookmark 1
© 2011 Kathleen Leatherwood

That Crazy English *th*

Kathleen Leatherwood

Note: When reading the individual letter sounds,
lowercase letters denote the *sound* as in the example word, and
UPPERCASE letters denote the *letter name* as in the alphabet.

2. t t t is the sound in tick
   h h h is the sound in hick
   But if thick is what you want to write
   You've got to have a th to make it right.

NOTE: use the voiced **th** sound in **that** for verse 1 and refrain
and the unvoiced **th** sound in **thick** for verse 2 and refrain

That Crazy English *th*
Lyrics

Note: When reading the individual letter sounds,
lowercase letters denote the *sound* as in the example word, and
UPPERCASE letters denote the *letter name* as in the alphabet.

NOTE: Use the voiced **th** sound in **that** for verse 1 & refrain
Use the unvoiced **th** sound in **thick** for verse 2 & refrain

Verses:

t t t is the sound in **tap**

h h h is the sound in **hat**

But if **that** is what you want to write

You've got to have a **th** to make it right.

t t t is the sound in **tick**

h h h is the sound in **hick**

But if **thick** is what you want to write

You've got to have a **th** to make it right.

Refrain:

th th th is the sound in **that (thick)**

But you need **two letters** to sound that way.

t and h are the usual sounds

But **together** they don't **sound** the same.

That Crazy English *th*
Chords

Note: **When reading the individual letter sounds,**
lowercase letters denote the *sound* as in the example word, and
UPPERCASE letters denote the *letter name* as in the alphabet.

Verse 1:

D   A7
t t t is the sound in **tap**

A7   D
h h h is the sound in **hat**

       G   D
But if **that** is what you want to write

      A7
You've got to have a **th** to

A7   D
make it right.

NOTE: Use the voiced **th** sound in **that**
for Verse 1 & Refrain

Use the unvoiced **th** sound in **thick**
for Verse 2 & Refrain

Verse 2:

D   A7
t t t is the sound in **tick**

A7   D
h h h is the sound in **hick**

       G   D
But if **thick** is what you want to write

      A7
You've got to have a **th** to

A7   D
make it right.

Refrain:

G   D
th th th is the sound in **that**
(thick)

        A7
But you need **two letters** to

  D
sound that way.
G   D
t and **h** are the usual sounds

      A7   A7   A7
But **together** they don't **sound**

      D
the same.

That Crazy English *sh*

Kathleen Leatherwood

Note: When reading the individual letter sounds,
lowercase letters denote the *sound* as in the example word, and
UPPERCASE letters denote the *letter name* as in the alphabet.

That Crazy English *sh*
Lyrics

Note: When reading the individual letter sounds, lowercase letters denote the *sound* as in the example word, and UPPERCASE letters denote the *letter name* as in the alphabet.

Verse:

s   s   s   is the sound in **sip**

h   h   h   is the sound in **hip**

But if **ship** is what you want to write

You've got to have a **sh** to make it right.

Refrain:

sh   sh   sh is the sound in **ship**

But you need **two letters** to sound that way.

s and **h** are the usual sounds

But **together** they don't **sound** the same.

That Crazy English *sh*
Chords

Note: When reading the individual letter sounds,
lowercase letters denote the *sound* as in the example word, and
UPPERCASE letters denote the *letter name* as in the alphabet.

Verse:

D   A7
s   s   s is the sound in **sip**

A7   D
h   h   h is the sound in **hip**

           G   D
But if **ship** is what you want to

           A7
You've got to have a **sh** to

A7   D
make it right.

Refrain:

G   D
sh sh sh is the sound in

ship

               A7
But you need **two letters** to

     D
sound that way.

G   D
s and **h** are the usual sounds

             A7   A7   A7
But **together** they don't **sound**

          D
the same.

That Crazy English *ch*

Kathleen Leatherwood

Note: When reading the individual letter sounds,
lowercase letters denote the *sound* as in the example word, and
UPPERCASE letters denote the *letter name* as in the alphabet.

47

That Crazy English *ch*
Lyrics

Note: When reading the individual letter sounds,
lowercase letters denote the *sound* as in the example word, and
UPPERCASE letters denote the *letter name* as in the alphabet.

Verse:

c   c   c   is the sound in **cat**

h   h   h   is the sound in **hat**

But if **chat** is what you want to write

You've got to have a   **ch**   to make it right.

Refrain:

ch   ch   ch is the sound in **chat**

But you need two letters to sound that way.

c and **h** are the usual sounds

But **together** they don't **sound** the same.

That Crazy English *ch*
Chords

Note: When reading the individual letter sounds,
lowercase letters denote the *sound* as in the example word, and
UPPERCASE letters denote the *letter name* as in the alphabet.

Verse:

D   A7
c **c** **c** is the sound in **cat**

A7   D
h **h** **h** is the sound in **hat**

    G   D
But if **chat** is what you want to

write

    A7
You've got to have a **ch** to

A7   D
make it right.

Refrain:

G   D
ch **ch** **ch** is the sound in

chat

      A7
But you need two letters to

  D
sound that way.

G   D
c and **h** are the usual sounds

    A7 A7   A7
But **together** they don't **sound**

  D
the same.

That Crazy English *th, sh, ch*

Kathleen Leatherwood

Note: When reading the individual letter sounds,
lowercase letters denote the *sound* as in the example word, and
UPPERCASE letters denote the *letter name* as in the alphabet.

2.   s s s is the sound in sip
     h h h is the sound in hip
     But if ship is what you want to write
     You've got to have a sh to make it right.
  Refrain:
     sh sh sh is the sound in ship
     But you need two letters to sound that way.
     s and h are the usual sounds
     But together they don't sound the same.

3.   c c c is the sound in cat
     h h h is the sound in hat
     But if chat is what you want to write
     You've got to have a ch to make it right.
  Refrain:
     ch ch ch is the sound in chat
     But you need two letters to sound that way.
     c and h are the usual sounds
     But together they don't sound the same.

That Crazy English *th, sh, ch*
Lyrics

Note: When reading the individual letter sounds,
lowercase letters denote the *sound* as in the example word, and
UPPERCASE letters denote the *letter name* as in the alphabet.

Verse:

t t t is the sound in **tap**

h h h is the sound in **hat**

But if **that** is what you want to write

You've got to have a **th** to make it right.

Refrain:

th th th is the sound in **that**

But you need **two letters** to sound that way.

t and h are the usual sounds

But **together** they don't **sound** the same.

Verse:

t t t is the sound in **tick**

h h h is the sound in **hick**

But if **thick** is what you want to write

You've got to have a **th** to make it right.

Refrain:

th th th is the sound in **thick**

But you need **two letters** to sound that way.

t and h are the usual sounds

But **together** they don't **sound** the same.

Verse:

s s s is the sound in **sip**

h h h is the sound in **hip**

But if **ship** is what you want to write

You've got to have a **sh** to make it right.

Refrain:

sh sh sh is the sound in **ship**

But you need **two letters** to sound that way.

s and h are the usual sounds

But **together** they don't **sound** the same.

Verse:

c c c is the sound in **cat**

h h h is the sound in **hat**

But if **chat** is what you want to write

You've got to have a **ch** to make it right.

Refrain:

ch ch ch is the sound in **chat**

But you need **two letters** to sound that way.

c and h are the usual sounds

But **together** they don't **sound** the same.

51

That Crazy English *th, sh, ch*
Chords

Note: When reading the individual letter sounds,
lowercase letters denote the *sound* as in the example word, and
UPPERCASE letters denote the *letter name* as in the alphabet.

Verse 1:

D   A7
t t t is the sound in **tap**

A7   D
h h h is the sound in **hat**

     G   D
But if **that** is what you want to write

     A7
You've got to have a **th** to

A7   D
make it right.

NOTE: Use the voiced **th** sound in **that**
for Verse 1 & Refrain

Use the unvoiced **th** sound in **thick** for
Verse 2 & Refrain

Verse 2:

D   A7
t t t is the sound in **tick**

A7   D
h h h is the sound in **hick**

     G   D
But if **thick** is what you want to write

     A7
You've got to have a **th** to

A7   D
make it right.

Refrain:

G   D
th th th is the sound in **that (thick)**

     A7
But you need **two letters** to

  D
sound that way.

G   D
t and **h** are the usual sounds

    A7   A7   A7
But **together** they don't **sound**

  D
the same.

52

That Crazy English *th, sh, ch*
Chords

Note: When reading the individual letter sounds,
lowercase letters denote the *sound* as in the example word, and
UPPERCASE letters denote the *letter name* as in the alphabet.

Verse:

D   A7
s s s is the sound in **sip**

A7   D
h h h is the sound in **hip**

       G   D
But if **ship** is what you want to write
      A7
You've got to have a **sh** to

A7   D
make it right.

Refrain:

G   D
sh sh sh is the sound in **ship**

       A7
But you need **two letters** to
  D
sound that way.

G   D
s and **h** are the usual sounds

     A7   A7   A7
But **together** they don't **sound**
  D
the same.

Verse:

D   A7
c c c is the sound in **cat**

A7   D
h h h is the sound in **hat**

       G   D
But if **chat** is what you want to write
      A7
You've got to have a **ch** to

A7   D
make it right.

Refrain:

G   D
ch ch ch is the sound in **chat**

       A7
But you need two letters to
  D
sound that way.

G   D
c and **h** are the usual sounds

     A7   A7   A7
But **together** they don't **sound**
  D
the same.

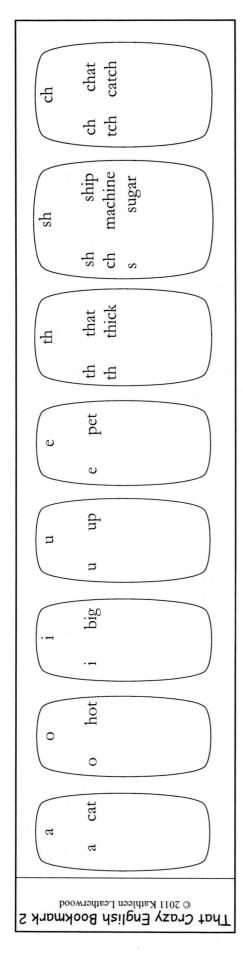
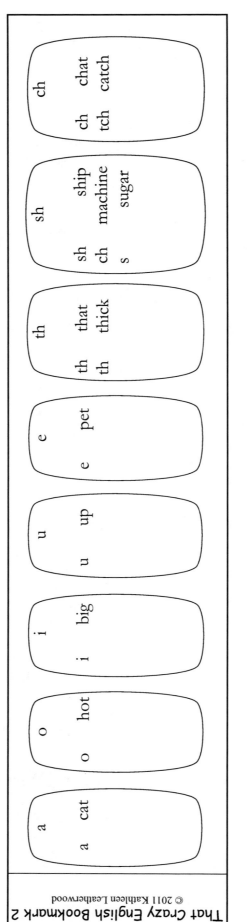
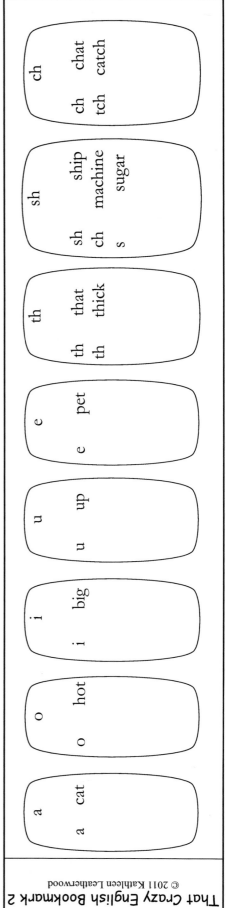

Bookmark 1:

ch — chat catch
ch tch

sh — ship machine sugar
sh ch s

th — that thick
th th

e — pet
e

u — up
u

i — big
i

o — hot
o

a — cat
a

Bookmark 2:

ch — chat catch
ch tch

sh — ship machine sugar
sh ch s

th — that thick
th th

e — pet
e

u — up
u

i — big
i

o — hot
o

a — cat
a

Bookmark 3:

ch — chat catch
ch tch

sh — ship machine sugar
sh ch s

th — that thick
th th

e — pet
e

u — up
u

i — big
i

o — hot
o

a — cat
a

That Crazy English *ow, ou*

Kathleen Leatherwood

Note: When reading the individual letter sounds,
lowercase letters denote the *sound* as in the example word, and
UPPERCASE letters denote the *letter name* as in the alphabet.

ow ow ow is the sound in wow   In cow and pow, and
ev - en how   But if out is what you want to write   You've
got to have O U   to ma-ke it right.   ow ow ow is the
sound in wow And ow ow ow is the sound in out.   Some-times let-ters
sound the same   But they don't al-ways lo-ok the same.

That Crazy English *ow, ou*
Lyrics

Note: When reading the individual letter sounds,
lowercase letters denote the *sound* as in the example word, and
UPPERCASE letters denote the *letter name* as in the alphabet.

Verse:

ow ow ow is the sound in **wow**

In **cow** and **pow**, and even **how**

But if **out** is what you want to write

You've got to have **O U** to make it right.

Refrain:

    ow ow ow is the sound in **wow** and

    ow ow ow is the sound in **out**.

    Sometimes letters **sound** the same

    But they don't always **look** the same.

That Crazy English *ow, ou*
Chords

Note: When reading the individual letter sounds,
lowercase letters denote the *sound* as in the example word, and
UPPERCASE letters denote the *letter name* as in the alphabet.

Verse:

D   A7
ow   ow   ow is the sound in
wow

   A7   A7   D
In **cow** and **pow** and even **how**

      G   D
But if **out** is what you want to
write
        A7
You've got to have **O U** to

 A7   D
make it right.

Refrain:

G   D
ow   ow   ow is the sound in

wow and

A7   D
ow   ow   ow is the sound in

out.

G   D
Sometimes letters **sound** the
same

        A7   A7   A7
But they don't always **look** the
  D
same.

57

That Crazy English *ow, ou*

Phono-Graphix Version

Kathleen Leatherwood

Note: When reading the individual letter sounds,
lowercase letters denote the *sound* as in the example word, and
UPPERCASE letters denote the *letter name* as in the alphabet.

That Crazy English *ow, ou*
Lyrics

Phono-Graphix Version

Note: When reading the individual letter sounds,
        lowercase letters denote the *sound* as in the example word, and
        UPPERCASE letters denote the *letter name* as in the alphabet.

Verse:

ow ow ow is the sound in **wow**

In **cow** and **pow**, and even **how**

But if **out** is what you want to write

You've got to have **O U** to make it right.

Refrain:

ow   ow   ow is the sound in **wow**, and

ow   ow   ow is the sound in **out**.

Some sound pictures **sound** the same

But they don't always **look** the same.

That Crazy English *ow, ou*
Chords

Phono-Graphix Version

Note: When reading the individual letter sounds,
lowercase letters denote the *sound* as in the example word, and
UPPERCASE letters denote the *letter name* as in the alphabet.

Verse:

D   A7
ow ow ow is the sound in
wow

     A7   A7   D
In **cow** and **pow**, and even **how**

           G   D
But if **out** is what you want to
write
          A7
You've got to have **O U** to

  A7   D
make it right.

Refrain:

G   D
ow ow ow is the sound in

wow and

 A7   D
ow ow ow is the sound in

out.

G   D
Some sound pictures **sound** the
same

          A7   A7   A7
But they don't always **look** the
         D
same.

That Crazy English *A*

Kathleen Leatherwood

Note: When reading the individual letter sounds,
lowercase letters denote the *sound* as in the example word, and
UPPERCASE letters denote the *letter name* as in the alphabet.

61

That Crazy English A
Lyrics

Note: When reading the individual letter sounds,
lowercase letters denote the *sound* as in the example word, and
UPPERCASE letters denote the *letter name* as in the alphabet.

Verse:

A A A is the sound in **day**

In **make** and **wait**, and even **say**

But which do you use when you want to write?

You've got to **use your eyes** to make it right.

Refrain:

   A A A is the sound in **day**

   But you have some choices you can make.

   A A A is the sound you hear

   But it doesn't always **look** the same.

That Crazy English *A*
Chords

Note: When reading the individual letter sounds,
lowercase letters denote the *sound* as in the example word, and
UPPERCASE letters denote the *letter name* as in the alphabet.

Verse:

D   A7
A A A   is the sound in **day**

     A7   D
In **make** and **wait** and even **say**

       G
But which do you use when you

   D
 want to write?

        A7
You've got to **use your eyes** to

A7   D
make it right.

Refrain:

G   D
A A A is the sound in **day**

             A7   D
But you have some choices you
can make.

G   D
A A A is the sound you hear

        A7   A7   A7
But it doesn't always **look**

      D
the same.

© 2009 Kathleen Leatherwood

63

That Crazy English *O*

Kathleen Leatherwood

Note: When reading the individual letter sounds,
lowercase letters denote the *sound* as in the example word, and
UPPERCASE letters denote the *letter name* as in the alphabet.

Verse

O O O is the sound in go__ In home and boat, and

ev - en slow But which do you use when you want to write? You've

Refrain

got to use your eyes to ma-ke it right. O O O is the

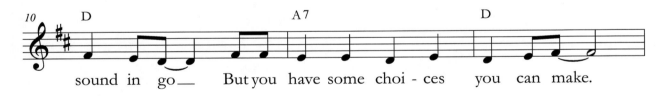

sound in go__ But you have some choi - ces you can make.

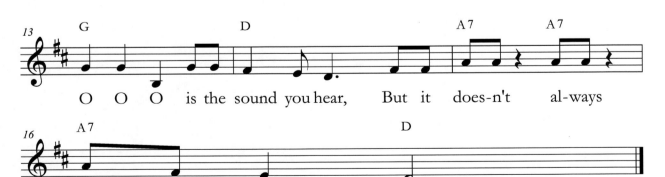

O O O is the sound you hear, But it does-n't al-ways

lo - ok the same.

That Crazy English O
Lyrics

Note: When reading the individual letter sounds,
lowercase letters denote the *sound* as in the example word, and
UPPERCASE letters denote the *letter name* as in the alphabet.

Verse:

O O O is the sound in **go**

In **home** and **boat**, and even **slow**

But which do you use when you want to write?

You've got to **use your eyes** to make it right.

Refrain:

O O O is the sound in **go**

But you have some choices you can make.

O O O is the sound you hear

But it doesn't always **look** the same.

That Crazy English *O*
Chords

Verse:

D   A7
O   O   O   is the sound in **go**

       A7   D
In **home** and **boat**, and even
slow

         G
But which do you use when you

    D
 want to write?

        G
You've got to **use your eyes** to

A7   D
make it right.

Refrain:

 G   D
O   O   O   is the sound in **go**

                A7   D
But you have some choices you
can make.

 G   D
O   O   O   is the sound you

hear,

            A7   A7   A7
But it doesn't always **look**

        D
the same.

That Crazy English *I*

Kathleen Leatherwood

Note: When reading the individual letter sounds,
lowercase letters denote the *sound* as in the example word, and
UPPERCASE letters denote the *letter name* as in the alphabet.

That Crazy English *I*
Lyrics

Note: When reading the individual letter sounds, lowercase letters denote the *sound* as in the example word, and UPPERCASE letters denote the *letter name* as in the alphabet.

Verse:

I I I is the sound in **hi**

In **right** and **bike**, and even **pie**

But which do you use when you want to write?

You've got to **use your eyes** to make it right.

Refrain:

> **I I I** is the sound in **hi**
>
> But you have some choices you can make.
>
> **I I I** is the sound you hear
>
> But it doesn't always **look** the same.

That Crazy English *I*
Chords

Verse:

D   A7
I I I is the sound in **hi**

   A7   D
In **right** and **kind**, and even **pie**

     G
But which do you use when you

  D
want to write?

     A7
You've got to **use your eyes** to
A7   D
make it right.

Refrain:

G   D
I I I is the sound in **hi**

        A7   D
But you have some choices you
can make.

G   D
I I I is the sound you hear

       A7   A7   A7
But it doesn't always **look**

     D
the same.

That Crazy English *U*

Kathleen Leatherwood

Note: When reading the individual letter sounds,
lowercase letters denote the *sound* as in the example word, and
UPPERCASE letters denote the *letter name* as in the alphabet.

Verse

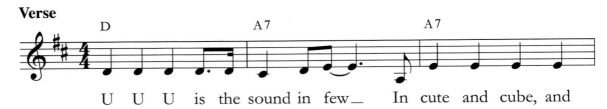

U U U is the sound in few__ In cute and cube, and

ev - en cue But which do you use when you want to write? You've

Refrain

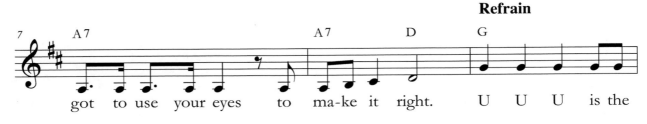

got to use your eyes to ma-ke it right. U U U is the

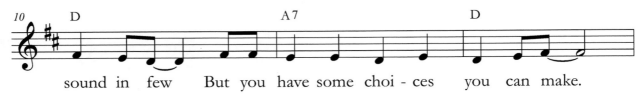

sound in few But you have some choi - ces you can make.

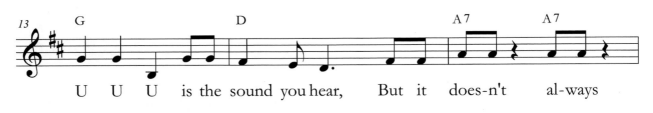

U U U is the sound you hear, But it does-n't al-ways

lo - ok the same.

That Crazy English *U*
Lyrics

Note: When reading the individual letter sounds, lowercase letters denote the *sound* as in the example word, and UPPERCASE letters denote the *letter name* as in the alphabet.

Verse:

U U U is the sound in **few**

In **cute** and **cube**, and even **cue**

But which do you use when you want to write?

You've got to **use your eyes** to make it right.

Refrain:

U U U is the sound in **few**

But you have some choices you can make.

U U U is the sound you hear

But it doesn't always **look** the same.

© 2009 Kathleen Leatherwood

That Crazy English *U*
Chords

Note: When reading the individual letter sounds, lowercase letters denote the *sound* as in the example word, and UPPERCASE letters denote the *letter name* as in the alphabet.

Verse:

D   A7
U U U is the sound in **few**

    A7   D
In **cute** and **cube**, and even **cue**

        G
But which do you use when you
  D
 want to write?

       A7
You've got to **use your eyes** to

A7   D
make it right.

Refrain:

G   D
U U U is the sound in **few**

            A7   D
But you have some choices you
can make.

G   D
U U U is the sound you

hear,

      A7   A7   A7
But it doesn't always **look**
    D
the same.

That Crazy English *E*

Kathleen Leatherwood

Note: When reading the individual letter sounds,
lowercase letters denote the *sound* as in the example word, and
UPPERCASE letters denote the *letter name* as in the alphabet.

73

That Crazy English *E*
Lyrics

Note: When reading the individual letter sounds,
lowercase letters denote the *sound* as in the example word, and
UPPERCASE letters denote the *letter name* as in the alphabet.

Verse:

E E E is the sound in **me**

In **sleep** and **piece**, and even **sea**

But which do you use when you want to write?

You've got to **use your eyes** to make it right.

Refrain:

E E E   is the sound in **me**

But you have some choices you can make.

E E E   is the sound you hear

But it doesn't always **look** the same.

That Crazy English *E*
Chords

Note: When reading the individual letter sounds,
lowercase letters denote the *sound* as in the example word, and
UPPERCASE letters denote the *letter name* as in the alphabet.

Verse:

D   A7
E   E   E is the sound in **me**

A7   D
In **sleep** and **piece** and even **sea**

         G
But which do you use when you

     D
   want to write?

         A7
You've got to **use your eyes** to

A7   D
make it right.

Refrain:

G   D
E   E   E is the sound in **me**

                A7   D
But you have some choices you
can make.

G   D
E   E   E is the sound you hear

          A7   A7   A7
But it doesn't always **look**

         D
the same.

That Crazy English *er*

Kathleen Leatherwood

Note: When reading the individual letter sounds,
lowercase letters denote the *sound* as in the example word, and
UPPERCASE letters denote the *letter name* as in the alphabet.

That Crazy English *er*
Lyrics

Note: When reading the individual letter sounds,
lowercase letters denote the *sound* as in the example word, and
UPPERCASE letters denote the *letter name* as in the alphabet.

Verse:

er   er   er is the sound in **word**

In **hurt** and **pert**, and even **herd**

Fir and **spur** and **her** all rhyme

But you use a different vowel, every time.

Refrain:

   er   er   er is the sound in **word**

   But it doesn't always **look** that way.

   Sometimes letters **sound** the same

   But they don't always **look** the same.

That Crazy English *er*
Chords

Note: When reading the individual letter sounds, lowercase letters denote the *sound* as in the example word, and UPPERCASE letters denote the *letter name* as in the alphabet.

Verse:

D   A7
er er er is the sound in **word**

     A7   D
In **hurt** and **pert** and even **herd**

G   D
Fir and **spur** and **her** all rhyme

        A7
But you use a different vowel

A7   D
every time.

Refrain:

G   D
er er er is the sound in **word**

             A7   D
But it doesn't always **look** that way.

G   D
Sometimes letters **sound** the same

       A7   A7   A7
But they don't always **look** the
      D
same.

That Crazy English *er*

Phono-Graphix Version

Kathleen Leatherwood

Note: When reading the individual letter sounds,
lowercase letters denote the *sound* as in the example word, and
UPPERCASE letters denote the *letter name* as in the alphabet.

That Crazy English *er*
Lyrics

Phono-Graphix Version

Note: When reading the individual letter sounds,
lowercase letters denote the *sound* as in the example word, and
UPPERCASE letters denote the *letter name* as in the alphabet.

Verse:

er er er is the sound in **word**

In **hurt** and **pert**, and even **herd**

Fir and **spur** and **her** all rhyme

But you use a different vowel, every time.

Refrain:

er er er is the sound in **word**

But it doesn't always **look** that way.

Some sound pictures **sound** the same

But they don't always **look** the same.

That Crazy English *er*
Chords

Phono-Graphix Version

Note: When reading the individual letter sounds,
lowercase letters denote the *sound* as in the example word, and
UPPERCASE letters denote the *letter name* as in the alphabet.

Verse:

D   A7
er   er   er   is the sound in **word**

    A7   D
In **hurt** and **pert** and even **herd**

G   D
Fir and **spur** and **her** all rhyme

       A7
But you use a different vowel

A7   D
every time.

Refrain:

G   D
er   er   er   is the sound in **word**

     A7   D
But it doesn't always **look** that
way.

G   D
Some sound pictures **sound** the
same

     A7   A7   A7
But they don't always **look** the
    D
same.

That Crazy English *oy*

Kathleen Leatherwood

Note: When reading the individual letter sounds,
lowercase letters denote the *sound* as in the example word, and
UPPERCASE letters denote the *letter name* as in the alphabet.

Verse

oy oy oy is the sound in boy— In toy and coy, and

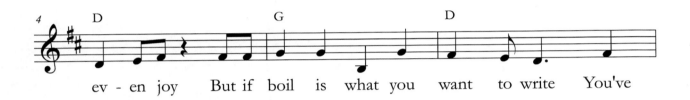

ev - en joy   But if boil is what you want to write   You've

Refrain

got to have O I to ma-ke it right.   oy oy oy is the sound in boy And

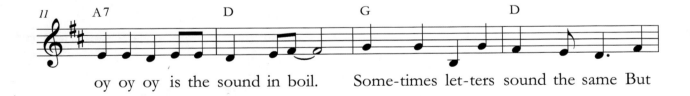

oy oy oy is the sound in boil.   Some-times let-ters sound the same But

they don't al - ways lo - ok the same.

That Crazy English *oy*
Lyrics

Note: **When reading the individual letter sounds,
lowercase letters denote the** *sound* **as in the example word, and**
UPPERCASE **letters denote the** *letter name* **as in the alphabet.**

Verse:

oy oy oy is the sound in **boy**

In **toy** and **coy**, and even **joy**

But if **boil** is what you want to write

You've got to have **O I** to make it right.

Refrain:

> **oy   oy   oy** is the sound in **boy** and
>
> **oy   oy   oy** is the sound in **boil.**
>
> Sometimes letters **sound** the same
>
> But they don't always **look** the same.

That Crazy English *oy*
Chords

Note: When reading the individual letter sounds,
lowercase letters denote the *sound* as in the example word, and
UPPERCASE letters denote the *letter name* as in the alphabet.

Verse:

D   A7
oy oy oy is the sound in **boy**

  A7   A7   D
In **toy** and **coy**, and even **joy**

        G   D
But if **boil** is what you want to
write

       A7
You've got to have **O I** to

A7   D
make it right.

Refrain:

G   D
oy oy   oy is the sound in **boy**

A7   D
And **oy oy   oy** is the sound
in **boil.**

G   D
Sometimes letters **sound** the
same

      A7   A7   A7
But they don't always **look** the
  D
same.

That Crazy English *oy*

Phono-Graphix Version

Kathleen Leatherwood

Note: When reading the individual letter sounds,
lowercase letters denote the *sound* as in the example word, and
UPPERCASE letters denote the *letter name* as in the alphabet.

Verse

oy oy oy is the sound in boy__ In toy and coy, and

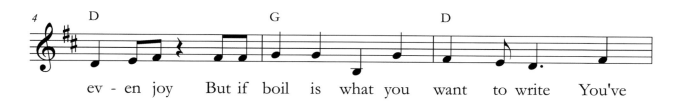

ev - en joy But if boil is what you want to write You've

Refrain

got to have O I to ma-ke it right. oy oy oy is the sound in boy And

oy oy oy is the sound in boil. Some sound pic - tures

sound the same, But they don't al - ways lo - ok the same.

85

That Crazy English - oy
Lyric Sheet

Phono-Graphix Version

Note: When reading the individual letter sounds,
lowercase letters denote the *sound* as in the example word, and
UPPERCASE letters denote the *letter name* as in the alphabet.

Verse:

oy oy oy is the sound in **boy**

In **toy** and **coy**, and even **joy**

But if **boil** is what you want to write

You've got to have **O I** to make it right.

Refrain:

    oy oy oy is the sound in **boy** and

    oy oy oy is the sound in **boil.**

    Some sound pictures **sound** the same

    But they don't always **look** the same.

That Crazy English *oy*
Chords

Phono-Graphix Version

Note: When reading the individual letter sounds,
lowercase letters denote the *sound* as in the example word, and
UPPERCASE letters denote the *letter name* as in the alphabet.

Verse:

D   A7
oy oy oy is the sound in **boy**

   A7   A7   D
In **toy** and **coy**, and even **joy**

           G   D
But if **boil** is what you want to
write

           A7
You've got to have **O I** to

A7   D
make it right.

Refrain:

G   D
oy oy   oy is the sound in **boy**

A7   D
And **oy oy   oy** is the sound
in **boil.**

G   D
Some sound pictures **sound** the
same,

       A7   A7   A7
But they don't always **look** the
    D
same.

That Crazy English *aw*

Kathleen Leatherwood

Note: When reading the individual letter sounds,
lowercase letters denote the *sound* as in the example word, and
UPPERCASE letters denote the *letter name* as in the alphabet.

Verse

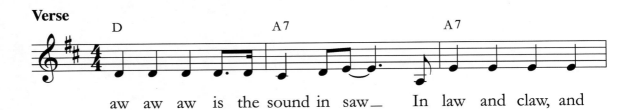

aw aw aw is the sound in saw— In law and claw, and

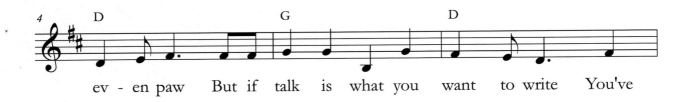

ev - en paw But if talk is what you want to write You've

Refrain

got to have A L to ma-ke it right. aw aw aw is the sound in saw And

aw aw aw is the sound in talk. Some-times let-ters sound the same But

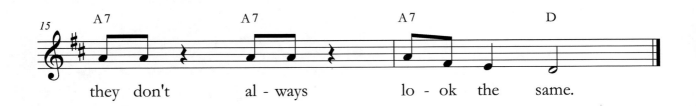

they don't al - ways lo - ok the same.

That Crazy English *aw*
Lyrics

Note: **When reading the individual letter sounds,**
lowercase letters denote the *sound* as in the example word, and
UPPERCASE letters denote the *letter name* as in the alphabet.

Verse:

aw aw aw is the sound in **saw**

In **law** and **claw**, and even **paw**

But if **talk** is what you want to write

You've got to have **A L** to make it right.

Refrain:

aw aw aw is the sound in **saw**

And **aw aw aw** is the sound in **talk**.

Sometimes letters **sound** the same

But they don't always **look** the same.

That Crazy English *aw*
Chords

Note: When reading the individual letter sounds, lowercase letters denote the *sound* as in the example word, and UPPERCASE letters denote the *letter name* as in the alphabet.

Verse:

D   A7
aw aw aw is the sound in **saw**

 A7   D
In **law** and **claw** and even **paw**

  G
But if **talk** is what you

 D
want to write

  A7
You've got to have **A L** to

A7 D
make it right.

Refrain:

G   D
aw aw aw is the sound in **saw**

    A7   D
And **aw aw aw** is the sound in **talk**.

G   D
Sometimes letters **sound** the

same

    A7   A7 A7
But they don't always **look**

    D
the same.

© 2011 Kathleen Leatherwood

90

That Crazy English *aw*

Phono-Graphix Version

Kathleen Leatherwood

Note: When reading the individual letter sounds,
lowercase letters denote the *sound* as in the example word, and
UPPERCASE letters denote the *letter name* as in the alphabet.

Verse

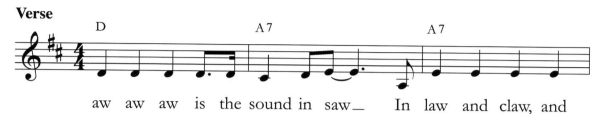

aw aw aw is the sound in saw— In law and claw, and

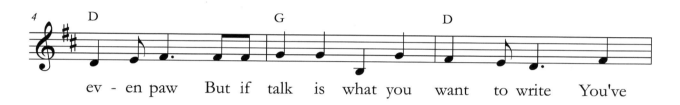

ev - en paw But if talk is what you want to write You've

Refrain

got to have A L to ma-ke it right. aw aw aw is the sound in saw And

aw aw aw is the sound in talk. Some sound pic - tures

sound the same But they don't al-ways lo-ok the same.

That Crazy English *aw*
Lyrics

Phono-Graphix Version

Note: When reading the individual letter sounds,
lowercase letters denote the *sound* as in the example word, and
UPPERCASE letters denote the *letter name* as in the alphabet.

Verse:

aw aw aw is the sound in **saw**

In **law** and **claw**, and even **paw**

But if **talk** is what you want to write

You've got to have **A L** to make it right.

Refrain:

> **aw aw aw** is the sound in **saw**
>
> And **aw aw aw** is the sound in **talk**.
>
> Some sound pictures **sound** the same
>
> But they don't always **look** the same.

That Crazy English *aw*
Chords

Phono-Graphix Version

Note: When reading the individual letter sounds,
lowercase letters denote the *sound* as in the example word, and
UPPERCASE letters denote the *letter name* as in the alphabet.

Verse:

D   A7
aw aw aw is the sound in **saw**

     A7   D
In **law** and **claw** and even **paw**

         G
But if **talk** is what you

D
want to write

        A7
You've got to have **A L** to

A7   D
make it right.

Refrain:

G   D
aw aw aw is the sound in **saw**

     A7   D
And **aw aw aw** is the sound in
talk.

G   D
Some sound pictures **sound** the

same

     A7   A7   A7
But they don't always **look**

     D
the same.

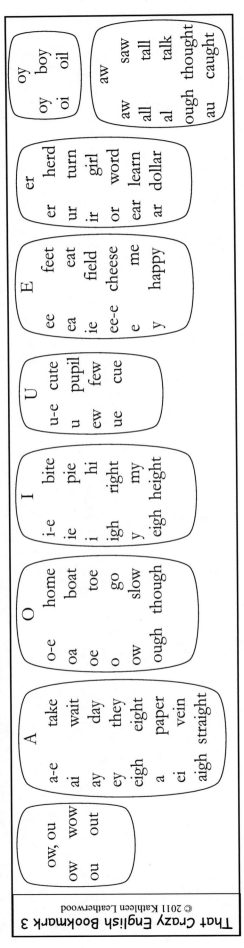

Bookmark 1

ow, ou — ow wow, ou out

A — a-e take, ai wait, ay day, ey they, eigh eight, a paper, ei vein, aigh straight

O — o-e home, oa boat, oe toe, o go, ow slow, ough though

I — i-e bite, ie pie, i hi, igh right, y my, eigh height

U — u-e cute, u pupil, ew few, ue cue

E — ee feet, ea eat, ie field, ee-e cheese, e me, y happy

er — er herd, ur turn, ir girl, or word, ear learn, ar dollar

oy — oy boy, oi oil

aw — aw saw, all tall, al talk, ough thought, au caught

That Crazy English Bookmark 3
© 2011 Kathleen Leatherwood

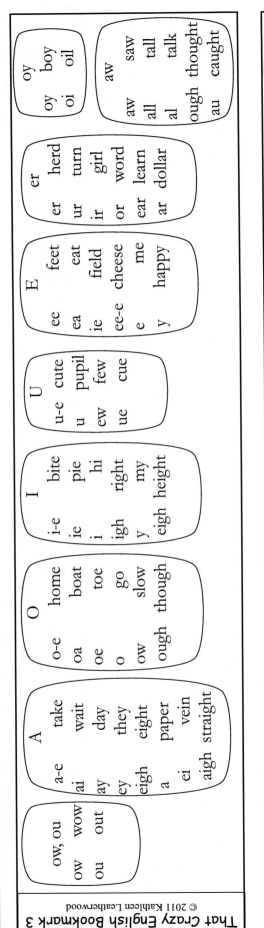

Bookmark 2

ow, ou — ow wow, ou out

A — a-e take, ai wait, ay day, ey they, eigh eight, a paper, ei vein, aigh straight

O — o-e home, oa boat, oe toe, o go, ow slow, ough though

I — i-e bite, ie pie, i hi, igh right, y my, eigh height

U — u-e cute, u pupil, ew few, ue cue

E — ee feet, ea eat, ie field, ee-e cheese, e me, y happy

er — er herd, ur turn, ir girl, or word, ear learn, ar dollar

oy — oy boy, oi oil

aw — aw saw, all tall, al talk, ough thought, au caught

That Crazy English Bookmark 3
© 2011 Kathleen Leatherwood

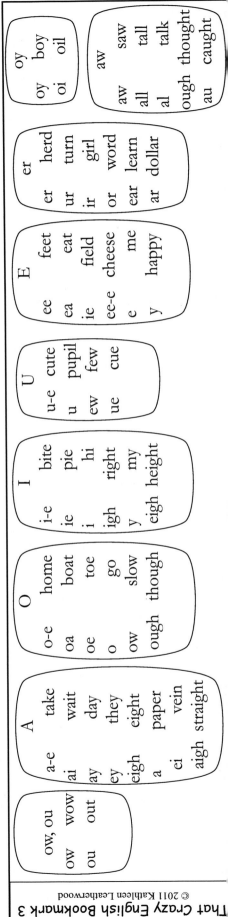

Bookmark 3

ow, ou — ow wow, ou out

A — a-e take, ai wait, ay day, ey they, eigh eight, a paper, ei vein, aigh straight

O — o-e home, oa boat, oe toe, o go, ow slow, ough though

I — i-e bite, ie pie, i hi, igh right, y my, eigh height

U — u-e cute, u pupil, ew few, ue cue

E — ee feet, ea eat, ie field, ee-e cheese, e me, y happy

er — er herd, ur turn, ir girl, or word, ear learn, ar dollar

oy — oy boy, oi oil

aw — aw saw, all tall, al talk, ough thought, au caught

That Crazy English Bookmark 3
© 2011 Kathleen Leatherwood

That Crazy English *O W*

Kathleen Leatherwood

Note: When reading the individual letter sounds,
lowercase letters denote the *sound* as in the example word, and
UPPERCASE letters denote the *letter name* as in the alphabet.

Verse

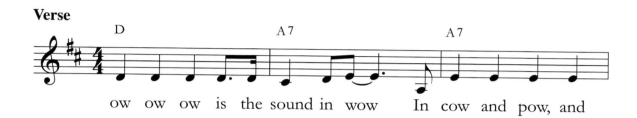

ow ow ow is the sound in wow   In cow and pow, and

ev-en how But if show is what you want to write, You need O W____ to

Refrain

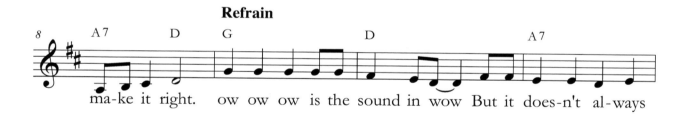

ma-ke it right.   ow ow ow is the sound in wow But it does-n't al-ways

sound that way   Some-times let - ters look the same   But

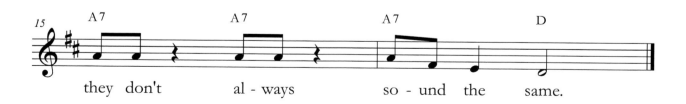

they don't   al - ways   so - und the   same.

That Crazy English *O W*
Lyrics

Note: When reading the individual letter sounds,
lowercase letters denote the *sound* as in the example word, and
UPPERCASE letters denote the *letter name* as in the alphabet.

Verse:

ow ow ow is the sound in **wow**

In **cow** and **pow**, and even **how**

But if **show** is what you want to write

You need **O W** to make it right.

Refrain:

ow ow ow is the sound in **wow**

But it doesn't always sound that way.

Sometimes letters **look** the same

But they don't always **sound** the same.

That Crazy English *O W*
Chords

Note: When reading the individual letter sounds,
      lowercase letters denote the *sound* as in the example word, and
      UPPERCASE letters denote the *letter name* as in the alphabet.

Verse:

D   A7
ow   **ow**   **ow**   is the sound in

wow

  A7   D
In **cow** and **pow** and even **how**

       G   D
But if **show** is what you want to
write

   A7   A7
You need **O W** to make

  D
it right.

Refrain:

G   D
ow   **ow**   **ow**   is the sound in

wow

      A7   D
But it doesn't always sound that
way.

G   D
Sometimes letters **look** the same

   A7   A7   A7
But they don't always **sound** the
   D
same.

That Crazy English *O W*

Phono-Graphix Version   Kathleen Leatherwood

Note: When reading the individual letter sounds,
lowercase letters denote the *sound* as in the example word, and
UPPERCASE letters denote the *letter name* as in the alphabet.

ow ow ow is the sound in wow   In cow and pow, and

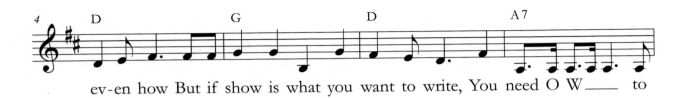

ev-en how But if show is what you want to write, You need O W____ to

Refrain

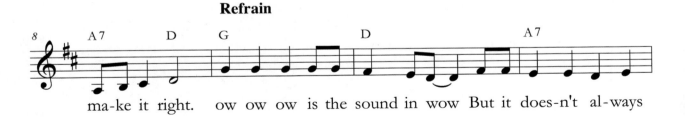

ma-ke it right.   ow ow ow is the sound in wow But it does-n't al-ways

sound that way   Some sound pic - tures   look the same   But

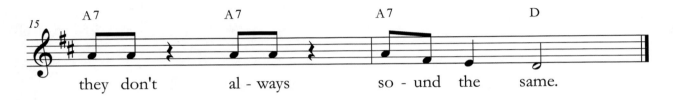

they don't   al - ways   so - und the   same.

That Crazy English *O W*
Lyrics

Phono-Graphix Version

Note: When reading the individual letter sounds,
lowercase letters denote the *sound* as in the example word, and
UPPERCASE letters denote the *letter name* as in the alphabet.

Verse:

ow ow ow is the sound in **wow**

In **cow** and **pow**, and even **how**

But if **show** is what you want to write

You need **O W** to make it right.

Refrain:

ow ow ow is the sound in **wow**

But it doesn't always sound that way.

Some sound pictures **look** the same

But they don't always **sound** the same.

That Crazy English *O W*
Chords

Phono-Graphix Version

Note: When reading the individual letter sounds, lowercase letters denote the *sound* as in the example word, and UPPERCASE letters denote the *letter name* as in the alphabet.

Verse:

D   A7
ow ow ow is the sound in

wow

 A7   D
In **cow** and **pow** and even **how**

   G   D
But if **show** is what you want to write

   A7   A7
You need **O W** to make

  D
it right.

Refrain:

G   D
ow ow ow is the sound in

wow

    A7   D
But it doesn't always sound that way.

 G   D
Some sound pictures **look** the same

    A7 A7 A7
But they don't always **sound** the
  D
same.

© 2009 Kathleen Leatherwood

That Crazy English *O O*

Kathleen Leatherwood

Note: When reading the individual letter sounds,
lowercase letters denote the *sound* as in the example word, and
UPPERCASE letters denote the *letter name* as in the alphabet.

Verse

oo oo oo is the sound in cool In pool and school, and

ev - en fool But if book is what you want to write You've

Refrain

got to have O O to ma-ke it right. oo oo oo is the

sound in cool (book) But it does-n't al-ways sound that way.

Some-times let - ters look the same But they don't al-ways

so - und the same.

2.   oo oo oo is the sound in book
    In look and took, and even foot
    But if boot is what you want to write
    You've got to have O O to make it right.

Refrain

That Crazy English *O O*
Lyrics

Note: When reading the individual letter sounds,
lowercase letters denote the *sound* as in the example word, and
UPPERCASE letters denote the *letter name* as in the alphabet.

Verses:

oo oo oo is the sound in **cool**

In **pool** and **school**, and even **fool**

But if **book** is what you want to write

You've got to have **O O** to make it right.

oo oo oo is the sound in **book**

In **look** and **took**, and even **foot**

But if **boot** is what you want to write

You've got to have **O O** to make it right.

Refrain:

oo oo oo is the sound in **cool (book)**

But it doesn't always sound that way.

Sometimes letters **look** the same

But they don't always **sound** the same.

That Crazy English *O O*
Chords

Note: When reading the individual letter sounds,
lowercase letters denote the *sound* as in the example word, and
UPPERCASE letters denote the *letter name* as in the alphabet.

Verse 1:

D   A7
oo   oo   oo   is the sound in **cool**

  A7   A7
In **pool** and **school**, and even **fool**

    G   D
But if **book** is what you want to write

   A7   A7   D
You've got to have **O O** to make it right

Verse 2:

D   A7
oo   oo   oo   is the sound in **book**

  A7   A7
In **look** and **took**, and even **foot**

    G   D
But if **boot** is what you want to write

   A7   A7   D
You've got to have **O O** to make it right

Refrain:

G   D
oo   oo   oo   is the sound in **cool (book)**

   A7   D
But it doesn't always sound that way.

G   D
Sometimes letters **look** the same

  A7   A7   A7   D
But they don't always **sound** the same.

That Crazy English *O O*

Phono-Graphix Version

Kathleen Leatherwood

Note: When reading the individual letter sounds,
lowercase letters denote the *sound* as in the example word, and
UPPERCASE letters denote the *letter name* as in the alphabet.

2. oo oo oo is the sound in book,
In look and took, and even foot
But if boot is what you want to write,
You've got to have O O to make it right.

Refrain

That Crazy English *O O*
Lyrics

Phono-Graphix Version

Note: **When reading the individual letter sounds,**
lowercase letters denote the *sound* as in the example word, and
UPPERCASE letters denote the *letter name* as in the alphabet.

Verses:

oo   oo   oo   is the sound in **cool**

In **pool** and **school**, and even **fool**

But if **book** is what you want to write

You've got to have **O O** to make it right.

oo   oo   oo   is the sound in **book**

In **look** and **took**, and even **foot**

But if **boot** is what you want to write

You've got to have **O O** to make it right.

Refrain:

oo   oo   oo   is the sound in **cool (book)**

But it doesn't always sound that way.

Some sound pictures **look** the same

But they don't always **sound** the same.

105

That Crazy English *O O*
Chords

Phono-Graphix Version

Note: When reading the individual letter sounds,
lowercase letters denote the *sound* as in the example word, and
UPPERCASE letters denote the *letter name* as in the alphabet.

Verse 1:

D   A7
oo   oo   oo is the sound in **cool**

   A7   A7
In **pool** and **school**, and even **fool**

        G   D
But if **book** is what you want to write

     A7   A7   D
You've got to have **O O** to make it right.

Verse 2:

D   A7
oo   oo   oo is the sound in **book**

      A7   A7
In **look** and **took**, and even **foot**

          G   D
But if **boot** is what you want to write

       A7   A7   D
You've got to have **O O** to make it right.

Refrain:

G   D
oo oo oo is the sound in **cool (book)**

       A7   D
But it doesn't always sound that way.

G   D
Some sound pictures **look** the same

     A7   A7   A7   D
But they don't always **sound** the same

That Crazy English *O U G H*

Kathleen Leatherwood

Note: When reading the individual letter sounds,
lowercase letters denote the *sound* as in the example word, and
UPPERCASE letters denote the *letter name* as in the alphabet.

Verse

aw aw aw is the sound in thought In fought and bought, and

ev - en cough But if through is what you want to write You need O U G H   to

Refrain

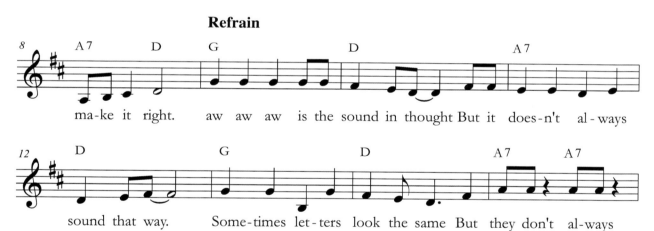

ma - ke it right.   aw aw aw is the sound in thought But it does-n't al - ways

sound that way.   Some-times let - ters look the same But they don't al - ways

so - und   the   same.

2. uf uf uf is the sound in rough
   In tough and even in enough
   But if though is what you want to write
   You need OUGH to make it right.

Refrain:

uf uf uf is the sound in rough
But it doesn't always sound that way.
Sometimes letters look the same
But they don't always sound the same.

That Crazy English *O U G H*
Lyrics

Note: When reading the individual letter sounds,
lowercase letters denote the *sound* as in the example word, and
UPPERCASE letters denote the *letter name* as in the alphabet.

Verse 1:

aw aw aw is the sound in **thought**

In **fought** and **bought**, and even **cough**

But if **through** is what you want to write

You need **O U G H** to make it right.

Verse 2:

uf uf uf is the sound in **rough**

In **tough** and even in **enough**

But if **though** is what you want to write

You need O U G H to make it right.

Refrain:

aw aw aw is the sound in **thought**

But it doesn't always sound that way.

Sometimes letters **look** the same

But they don't always **sound** the same.

Refrain:

uf uf uf is the sound in rough

But it doesn't always sound that way.

Sometimes letters **look** the same

But they don't always **sound** the same.

That Crazy English *O U G H*

Chords

Note: When reading the individual letter sounds,
lowercase letters denote the *sound* as in the example word, and
UPPERCASE letters denote the *letter name* as in the alphabet.

Verse 1:

D   A7
aw aw aw is the sound in **thought**

    A7   D
In **fought** and **bought**, and even **cough**

    G   D
But if **through** is what you want to write

   A7   A7   D
You need **O U G H** to make it right.

Verse 2:

D   A7
uf uf uf is the sound in **rough**

    A7   D
In **tough** and even in **enough**

    G   D
But if **though** is what you want to write

   A7   A7   D
You need **O U G H** to make it right.

Refrain:

G   D
aw aw aw is the sound in **thought**

    A7   A7
But it doesn't always sound that way.

G   D
Sometimes letters **look** the same

   A7   A7   A7   D
But they don't always **sound** the same.

Refrain:

G   D
uf uf uf is the sound in **rough**

    A7   A7
But it doesn't always sound that way.

G   D
Sometimes letters **look** the same

   A7   A7   A7   D
But they don't always **sound** the same.

That Crazy English *O U G H*

Phono-Graphix Version

Kathleen Leatherwood

Note: When reading the individual letter sounds,
lowercase letters denote the *sound* as in the example word, and
UPPERCASE letters denote the *letter name* as in the alphabet.

Verse

aw aw aw is the sound in thought In fought and bought, and

ev - en cough But if through is what you want to write, You need O U G H to

Refrain

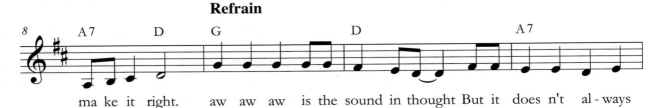

ma ke it right. aw aw aw is the sound in thought But it does n't al - ways

sound that way. Some sound pic - tures look the same but they don't al - ways

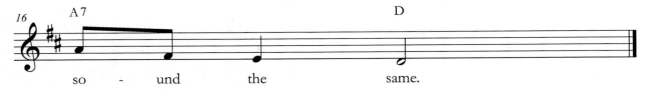

so - und the same.

2. uf uf uf is the sound in rough
In tough and even in enough
But if though is what you want to write
You need OUGH to make it right.

Refrain:

uf uf uf is the sound in rough
But it doesn't always sound that way.
Some sound pictures look the same
But they don't always sound the same.

That Crazy English *O U G H*
Lyrics

Phono-Graphix Version

Note: When reading the individual letter sounds,
lowercase letters denote the *sound* as in the example word, and
UPPERCASE letters denote the *letter name* as in the alphabet.

Verse 1:

aw aw aw is the sound in **thought**

In **fought** and **bought**, and even **cough**

But if **through** is what you want to write

You need **O U G H** to make it right.

Verse 2:

uf uf uf is the sound in **rough**

In **tough** and even in **enough**

But if **though** is what you want to write

You need O U G H to make it right.

Refrain:

aw aw aw is the sound in **thought**

But it doesn't always sound that way.

Some sound pictures **look** the same

But they don't always **sound** the same.

Refrain:

uf uf uf is the sound in **rough**

But it doesn't always sound that way.

Some sound pictures **look** the same

But they don't always **sound** the same.

That Crazy English *O U G H*
Chords

Phono-Graphix Version

Note: When reading the individual letter sounds,
lowercase letters denote the *sound* as in the example word, and
UPPERCASE letters denote the *letter name* as in the alphabet.

Verse 1:

D   A7
aw aw aw is the sound in **thought**

   A7   D
In **fought** and **bought**, and even **cough**

        G   D
But if **through** is what you want to write

   A7   A7 D
You need **O U G H** to make it right.

Refrain:

 G   D
aw aw aw is the sound in **thought**

     A7   A7
But it doesn't always sound that way.

G   D
Some sound pictures **look** the same

  A7   A7   A7   D
But they don't always **sound** the same.

Verse 2:

D   A7
uf uf uf is the sound in **rough**

   A7   D
In **tough** and even in **enough**

        G   D
But if **though** is what you want to write

   A7   A7 D
You need **O U G H** to make it right.

Refrain:

 G   D
uf uf uf is the sound in **rough**

     A7   A7
But it doesn't always sound that way.

G   D
Some sound pictures **look** the same

  A7   A7   A7   D
But they don't always **sound** the same.

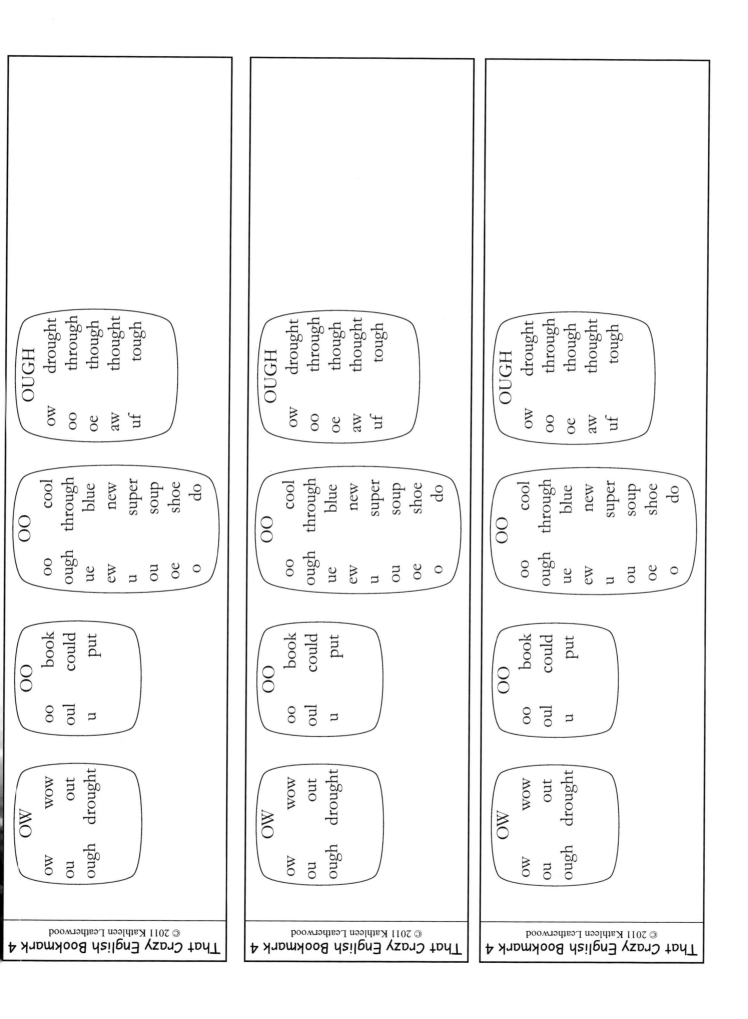

Bookmark 1

OW
ow — wow
ou — out
ough — drought

OO
oo — book
oul — could
u — put

OO
oo — cool
ough — through
ue — blue
ew — new
u — super
ou — soup
oe — shoe
o — do

OUGH
ow — drought
oo — through
oe — though
aw — thought
uf — tough

Bookmark 2

OW
ow — wow
ou — out
ough — drought

OO
oo — book
oul — could
u — put

OO
oo — cool
ough — through
ue — blue
ew — new
u — super
ou — soup
oe — shoe
o — do

OUGH
ow — drought
oo — through
oe — though
aw — thought
uf — tough

Bookmark 3

OW
ow — wow
ou — out
ough — drought

OO
oo — book
oul — could
u — put

OO
oo — cool
ough — through
ue — blue
ew — new
u — super
ou — soup
oe — shoe
o — do

OUGH
ow — drought
oo — through
oe — though
aw — thought
uf — tough

Reading Songs

My Reading Strategies Primary
My Reading Strategies Intermediate
The Parts of a Story

The Reading Songs Guide

Several years ago, I had been working on reading strategies with my English Language Learner (ELL) students and noticed their hesitation in applying the strategies without being prompted. At times they continued reading in spite of making mistakes or stopped and waited to see if I would supply the word. My main goal is always for students to gain independence in reading, and I kept thinking about how I could inspire them to monitor their reading by themselves. The result was the "My Reading Strategies—Primary" song. I believed if they just stopped in their tracks and thought about what they could do, they would solve their own problems. I brought the song to class. We spoke the words, sang them, and then talked about the strategies that we had already covered in our reading classes.

The song was put to the test at the end of the school year when our spring reading assessments were administered. One of my newest students, Rebecca, who had arrived in third grade from Denmark in the fall, speaking no English, was taking the Developmental Reading Assessment (DRA) with me. On the first page, she stopped in the middle of a sentence. I waited, hoping she would solve the problem on her own. I knew that if I simply told her the word, the error would not only count against her on the assessment but also not help her to solve any further problems she encountered. The test was also timed, so I knew that I had to make a decision within a few seconds. I took a risk. "Do you remember your song?" I asked. Rebecca started softly humming the tune, and her face lit up, "I can skip the word and go back!" I just smiled and said, "Hmm," as she continued reading, fixing the problem. I was amazed as she continued her assessment and passed, having solved her own problems along the way. That's when I started thinking that there may be something to setting helpful tips to music.

The reading raps/songs were written as reminders of strategies students learn during reading workshop. The primary reading strategies covered are
- look at the pictures
- say the first sound
- think of a look-alike (a word you know that looks similar)
- read, skip, reread (skip the word you don't know, continue reading, then go back and reread the entire sentence)
- break into parts (break a longer word into smaller parts)
- think about the story

These strategies are used primarily in **grades 1–3** but may also be used with students of other ages who have limited literacy, including speakers of other languages.

The intermediate reading strategies covered are
- think (activate prior knowledge)
- connect (make a connection to your own life)
- visualize (get a picture in your head of what is happening)

- question (ask yourself probing questions about what you are reading)
- infer (use what you already know plus the clues the author gives you to understand what you are reading)
- use fix-up strategies (these could be the primary reading strategies or whatever works when you are not understanding what you are reading)
- determine importance (know the difference between minor details and larger concepts: the big ideas)

These strategies are used from **grades 3–adult**, although some may also be used with primary students.

I like to start the school year, regardless of grade level, by making a classroom chart of "What Good Readers Do." This provides a baseline of what students are already doing when they read and a starting point for which strategies to teach them that are not mentioned. As the class learns a new strategy, it is added to the chart. Each strategy involves a large group lesson using a picture book or piece of writing for the teacher to model for the students. Appropriate books for reading strategies are available from a variety of language arts experts. Sources I have successfully used are listed in the Resources section at the end of this book. After the lesson is given, students practice the strategy with a book at their reading level and then share their experiences in the whole group.

The songs and bookmarks should be used after the strategy is taught; the students may color in the bookmark to indicate which strategies have been covered. Rebecca, the student who showed me that these songs could prove useful to readers, illustrated the primary bookmark. She chose graphics that would visually remind students of the strategy, such as the girl skipping with an arrow going back to the text for Read-Skip-Reread. As you plan your strategy lessons, discuss the actual graphics for the primary bookmark so the students can remember the strategies visually.

The intermediate bookmark has space for students to draw their own graphics. Students can draw a face for the strategies that show speech balloons. Inside the balloon, they can place a picture or a few appropriate words as a reminder. *Infer* could show a book + me and a light bulb for understanding. *Synthesize* could show some parts that make a whole when put together, like a puzzle. Your students will no doubt think of their own creative ways to remember each strategy.

"The Parts of a Story" was written to assist the students while they are reading and retelling or discussing a narrative text. This rap covers question words along with the typical retelling vocabulary that accompanies fiction writing: character, setting, problem, solution, and sequencing words. The word cards may be sorted and used when retelling a story or for prompting questions about the story.

I hope you and your students find these raps/songs as engaging and useful as my students have.

Reading Strategies Lesson: Primary

Materials

- Chart paper, chalkboard, white board, or SMART Board
- "What Good Readers Do" class chart
- Big book or picture book for modeling strategies
- Copy of "My Reading Strategies—Primary" lyrics in large format (overhead, chart paper, etc.). If you are only using one verse, cover up the verses not being used.

Large Group Lesson (15–20 minutes, depending on if you already have a chart made)

Use this lesson when you have already covered one or two reading strategies that are in the song. If you have not yet made a class chart, this would be a good time to start one. If you have a chart already, add strategies to it as students are ready. "Today we're going to talk about what good readers do and learn a song to help you remember your reading strategies. Let's look at the chart (or let's make a chart) about what good readers do to make sure that they understand what the author is saying." Read the strategies you have and solicit ideas from students, clarifying and tweaking to add the desired strategies to the chart. If students cannot think of any, use a big book or picture book think-aloud to model a strategy. You may only be using the beginning of the song and the first verse, or you can wait until you've covered all the strategies to introduce the song. "Now let's look at the words of the song." Read through the song, line by line, talking through the meaning of the lyrics, as shown below. Keep the "Good Readers" chart visible to the class as well.

I was reading one day, not too fast, not too slow.
"What happens if we read too quickly? Too slowly?" Talk about reading with expression, "like we talk," so the words make sense together.
And I came to a word that I didn't know.
"What can you do if you don't know a word?" (Students may refer to the chart.) "Let's see what this reader did."
I stopped in my tracks and started to shout. (Help!)
It's important that students are aware when they don't know a word and that it may prevent them from understanding the story. Learning to stop and think about what they can do will help them become more independent readers. "Why did this reader start to shout 'help'? How many of you just want someone to tell you the word so you can keep reading? Let's see what happens next."
But I took a little time to figure it out.
I didn't know the word, but I knew what to do.
I used my strategies, and I'll share them with you.
"Let's see what strategies this reader is going to try."

Continue reading through the words of the song, using as many verses as strategies you have covered. If you are not using all the verses, you can skip to the closing: "So if you're reading one day …" Read through the same parts of the song again with everyone reading along. I like to use a cloze technique when doing this, leaving out the last word of each line to let the students fill it in. This helps them become aware of the rhyming (which aids in remembering the words) and also helps slower readers catch up.

After the second reading, have students ask the person next to them what strategies he or she is going to try when reading. After a couple minutes, have them share their partner's idea in the large group.

Tell students that they will be learning more reading strategies, and they will practice with their own books. During the next session, you may want to add the melody and have the class sing the words. They may also want to rap the words hip-hop style with movements.

My Reading Strategies
Primary

Kathleen Leatherwood

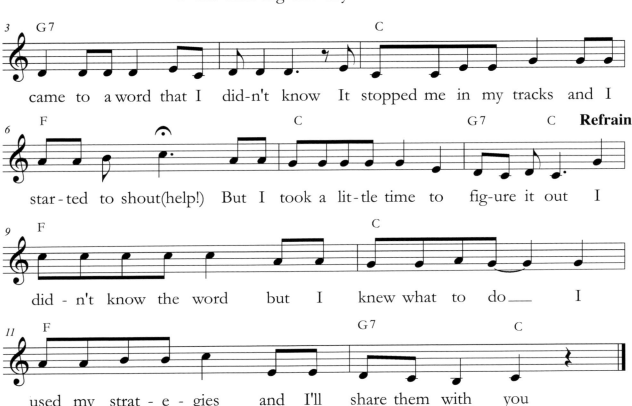

2. Does the picture help?
   Did I say the first sound?
   Does it look like a word
   That I've seen around?

   It stopped me in my tracks
   And I started to shout
   But I took a little time
   To figure it out

   Refrain

3. I can skip it right now
   And go back and reread
   I can break it into parts
   With lightning speed

I thought about the story
And I started to shout (yay!)
'Cause with a little time
I figured it out!

Refrain:

I didn't know the word
But I knew what to do
I used my strategies
And the meaning came through

4. So if you're reading one day
   Not too fast, not too slow
   And you come to a word
   That you don't know

   You can stop in your tracks
   No need to shout
   Just take a little time
   To figure it out

   CODA (Refrain melody):

   You may not know the word
   But you know what to do
   Just use your strategies
   And the meaning comes through

My Reading Strategies
Primary
Lyrics

1. I was reading one day
   Not too fast, not too slow
   And I came to a word
   That I didn't know
   It stopped me in my tracks
   And I started to shout (help!)
   But I took a little time
   To figure it out

Refrain:

**I didn't know the word
   But I knew what to do
I used my strategies
   And I'll share them with you**

2. Does the picture help?
   Did I say the first sound?
   Does it look like a word
   That I've seen around?
   It stopped me in my tracks
   And I started to shout
   But I took a little time
   To figure it out

Refrain

3. I can skip it right now
   And go back and reread
   I can break it into parts
   With lightning speed

I thought about the story
   And I started to shout (yay!)
'Cause with a little time
   I figured it out!

Refrain:

**I didn't know the word
   But I knew what to do
I used my strategies
   And the meaning came through**

4. So if you're reading one day
   Not too fast, not too slow
   And you come to a word
   That you don't know
   You can stop in your tracks
   No need to shout
   Just take a little time
   To figure it out

**CODA: (refrain melody)
   You may not know the word
      But you know what to do
Just use your strategies
      And the meaning comes
      through**

My Reading Strategies
Primary
Chords

    C   F   C
1. I was reading one day not too fast, not too slow
    G7   G7
  And I came to a word that I didn't know
   C   F
  It stopped me in my tracks and I started to shout (help!)
    C   G7 C
  But I took a little time to figure it out

Refrain:
 F   C
I didn't know the word but I knew what to do
 F   G7   C
I used my strategies, and I'll share them with you

     C   F   C
2. Does the picture help? Did I say the first sound?
    G7   G7
  Does it look like a word that I've seen around?
   C   F
  It stopped me in my tracks and I started to shout
    C   G7 C
  But I took a little time to figure it out

  Refrain

My Reading Strategies
Primary
Chords

       C   F   C

3. I can skip it right now and go back and reread

        G7   G7

I can break it into parts with lightning speed

     C   F

I thought about the story and I started to shout (yay!)

         C   G7   C

'Cause with a little time I figured it out!

Refrain:

    F   C

I didn't know the word but I knew what to do

    F   G7   C

I used my strategies, and the meaning came through

            C   F   C

4. So if you're reading one day not too fast, not too slow

        G7   G7

And you come to a word that you don't know

         C   F

You can stop in your tracks, no need to shout

     C   G7   C

Just take a little time to figure it out

CODA: (refrain melody)

      F   C

You may not know the word, but you know what to do

      F   G7   C

Just use your strategies, and the meaning comes through

6 Strategies for Good Readers
Primary

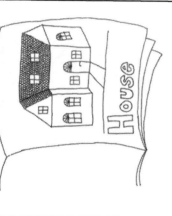
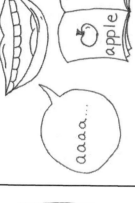

Look at the pictures

Say the first sound

Think of a look alike

---

6 Strategies for Good Readers
Primary

© 2010 Kathleen Leatherwood
Images © 2011 Rebecca Grundahl

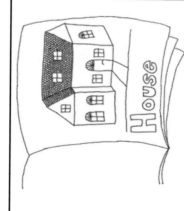
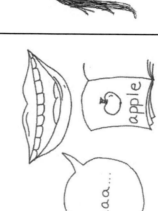
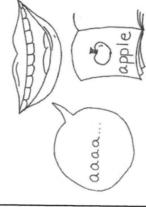

Look at the pictures

Say the first sound

Think of a look alike

---

6 Strategies for Good Readers
Primary

© 2010 Kathleen Leatherwood
Images © 2011 Rebecca Grundahl

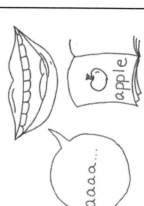
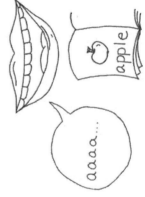
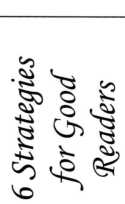

Look at the pictures

Say the first sound

Think of a look alike

Think about the story

Fan tas tic

Break into parts

Read, skip, reread

6 Strategies for Good Readers

Primary

© 2010 Kathleen Leatherwood
Images © 2011 Rebecca Grundahl

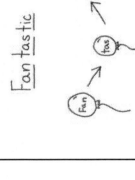

Think about the story

Fan tas tic

Break into parts

Read, skip, reread

6 Strategies for Good Readers

Primary

© 2010 Kathleen Leatherwood
Images © 2011 Rebecca Grundahl

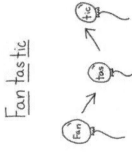

Think about the story

Fan tas tic

Break into parts

Read, skip, reread

6 Strategies for Good Readers

Primary

© 2010 Kathleen Leatherwood
Images © 2011 Rebecca Grundahl

Reading Strategies Lesson: Intermediate

Materials

- Chart paper, chalkboard, white board, or SMART Board
- "What Good Readers Do" class chart
- Big book or picture book for modeling strategies
- Copy of "My Reading Strategies–Intermediate" lyrics in large format (overhead, chart paper, etc.). If you are only using one verse, cover up the verses not being used

Large Group Lesson (15–20 minutes, depending on if you already have a chart made)

Use this lesson when you have already covered one or two reading strategies that are in the song. If you have not yet made a class chart, this would be a good time to start one. If you have a chart already, add strategies to it as students are ready. "Today we're going to talk about what good readers do and learn a song to help you remember your reading strategies. Let's look at the chart (or let's make a chart) about what good readers do to make sure that they understand what the author is saying." Read the strategies you have and solicit ideas from students, clarifying and tweaking to add the desired strategies to the chart. If students cannot think of any, use a big book or picture book think-aloud to model a strategy. You may only be using the beginning of the song and the first verse, or you can wait until you've covered all the strategies to introduce the song. "Now let's look at the words of the song." Read through the song, line by line, talking through the meaning of the lyrics, as shown below. Keep the Good Readers chart visible to the class as well.

I was reading one day, not too fast, not too slow.
"What happens if we read too quickly? Too slowly?" Talk about reading with expression, "like we talk," so the words make sense together. This is especially important with longer texts.
And I didn't understand what the author meant to show.
"What can you do if you don't understand the story?" (Students may refer to the chart.) "Let's see what this reader did."
I thought about the story and I started to shout (Help!)
It's important that students are aware when they stop understanding what they're reading. Learning to stop and think about what they can do will help them become more independent and thoughtful readers. "Why did this reader start to shout 'help'? Let's see what happens next."
But I took a little time to figure it out.
I didn't understand, but I knew what to do.
I used my strategies, and I'll share them with you.
"Let's see what strategies this reader is going to try."

Continue reading through the words of the song, using as many verses as strategies you have covered. If you are not using all the verses, you can skip to the closing: "I didn't understand …" Read through the same parts of the song again with everyone reading along. I like to use a cloze technique when doing this, leaving out the last word of each line and letting the students fill it in. This helps them become aware of the rhyming (which aids in remembering the words) and also helps slower readers catch up.

After the second reading, have students ask the person next to them what strategies he or she is going to try when reading. After a couple minutes, have them share their partner's idea in the large group.

Tell students that they will be learning more reading strategies, and they will practice with their own books. During the next session, you may want to add the melody and have the class sing the words. They may also want to rap the words hip-hop style with movements.

My Reading Strategies
Intermediate

Kathleen Leatherwood

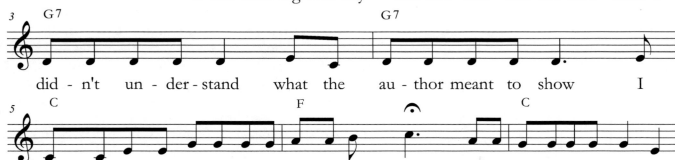

2. I asked myself questions about what I had read
   Then I got a good picture in my head
   I thought about the story and I started to shout
   But with a little time I figured it out!

3. I used the author's words, they were like a clue
   Then I thought about what I already knew
   I put it all together and I started to shout (Yay!)
   'Cause I learned to infer as I figured it out!

   Refrain

4. Then I thought even more about how and why,
   What the most important thing was for me to spy
   I made a connection to my own life
   And I figured it out without much strife

5. I thought about what happened from
      beginning to end
   How the characters went where the author led
   I put it all together and to my surprise
   I figured out how to synthesize!

   CODA (refrain melody)

   You may not understand
   But you know what to do
   Just use your strategies
   And the meaning comes through

My Reading Strategies
Intermediate
Lyrics

1. I was reading one day
     Not too fast, not too slow
   And I didn't understand
     What the author meant to show
   I thought about the story
     And I started to shout (help!)
   But I took a little time
     To figure it out

Refrain:
I didn't understand
   But I thought it all through
I used my strategies
   And I'll share them with you

2. I asked myself questions
     About what I had read
   Then I got a good picture
     In my head
   I thought about the story
     And I started to shout
   But with a little time
     I figured it out!

3. I used the author's words
     They were like a clue
   Then I thought about what
     I already knew
   I put it all together
     And I started to shout (Yay!)
   'Cause I learned to infer
     As I figured it out!

4. Then I thought even more
     About how and why
   What the most important thing
     Was for me to spy
   I made a connection
     To my own life
   And I figured it out
     Without much strife

Refrain

5. I thought about what happened
     From beginning to end
   How the characters went
     Where the author led
   I put it all together
     And to my surprise
   I figured out
     How to synthesize!

CODA (Refrain Melody)
   You may not understand
     But you know what to do
   Just use your strategies
     And the meaning comes
     through

My Reading Strategies
Intermediate
Chords

     C   F   C
1. I was reading one day not too fast, not too slow
     G7   G7
   And I didn't understand what the author meant to show
   C   F
   I thought about the story and I started to shout (Help!)
     C   G7 C
   But I took a little time to figure it out

   Refrain:
    F   C
   I didn't understand but I knew what to do
    F   G7   C
   I used my strategies, and I'll share them with you

     C   F   C
2. I asked myself questions about what I had read
     G7   G7
   Then I got a good picture in my head
   C   F
   I thought about the story and I started to shout
     C   G7 C
   But with a little time I figured it out!

       C   F C
3. I used the author's words, they were like a clue
     G7   G7
   Then I thought about what I already knew
   C   F
   I put it all together and I started to shout (Yay!)
     C   G7   C
   'Cause I learned to infer as I figured it out!

128

My Reading Strategies
Intermediate
Chords

                C   F   C

4. Then I thought even more about how and why

        G7   G7

What the most important thing was for me to spy

   C   F

I made a connection to my own life

        C   G7   C

And I figured it out without much strife

Refrain

    C   F   C

5. I thought about what happened from beginning to end

        G7   G7

How the characters went where the author led

  C   F

I put it all together and to my surprise

  C   G7   C

I figured out how to synthesize!

CODA (Refrain Melody)

        F   C

You may not understand, but you know what to do

  F   G7   C

Just use your strategies, and the meaning comes through

Card 1

8 Strategies for Good Readers

Intermediate

© 2011 Kathleen Leatherwood

I already know…

Think

That reminds me of…

Connect

Visualize

How? Why? Who?

Question

Card 2

8 Strategies for Good Readers

Intermediate

© 2011 Kathleen Leatherwood

I already know…

Think

That reminds me of…

Connect

Visualize

How? Why? Who?

Question

Card 3

8 Strategies for Good Readers

Intermediate

© 2011 Kathleen Leatherwood

I already know…

Think

That reminds me of…

Connect

Visualize

How? Why? Who?

Question

Hmm... what's most important?

Determine importance

Use Fix-up strategies

Synthesize

Infer

+ me =

Hmm... what's most important?

Determine importance

Use Fix-up strategies

Synthesize

Infer

+ me =

© 2011 Kathleen Leatherwood

Hmm... what's most important?

Determine importance

Use Fix-up strategies

Synthesize

Infer

+ me =

© 2011 Kathleen Leatherwood

The Parts of a Story

This rap can be done as a conga line dance.

Refrain:

Who, what, when, where, why, how?
Who, what, when, where, why, how?
Who, what, when, where, why, how?
What is the story about?

Verses:

1. **Who** is in the story?
   How will they change and grow?
   The **characters** will show us
   What we want to know.

2. **When** does the story happen?
   Where does it all take place?
   The **setting** is the story part
   Whose progress we can trace.

3. **How** do the characters feel now?
   How do they interact?
   How do they solve their **problem**
   And keep themselves intact?

4. **Why** do the characters act like that?
   What will they try to do?
   The **solution** to their problem
   Will reveal itself to you.

5. Who, what, when, where, why, how?
   We'll think along the way.
   The author shows us where to go
   And carries us away.

The Parts of a Story

Word Cards for Retelling

Beginning	Middle	End
First	Next	Then
After that	Finally	Characters
Setting	Problem	Solution
Who?	What?	When?
Where?	Why?	How?

Writing Songs

My Writing Form Tips

The Lowdown Rereading, Revising and Editing Blues

The Writing Songs Guide

The writing songs incorporate many features covered in standard writing workshops. "My Writing Form Tips" covers the organization of a topic and subtopics as well as attention to sentence structure, word choice, elaborated description, and a conclusion. It addresses planning for a piece of writing that fits into a one-paragraph or multi-paragraph format. The acronym, IDSEE ("Itsy") is a device to remind writers to introduce their topic (big idea, main idea), use precise words ("dazzle" words), use their senses to show detail (show, not tell), use varied sentence structures to explain their thoughts in detail, and to end with a conclusion. Be sure to stress to your writers that they are the most important readers they want to please and that they should challenge themselves to include all the IDSEE components as they are writing. Students who must write a five-paragraph essay for standardized tests, as well as those writing for other purposes, can use this structure. This stage of writing includes planning and drafting.

"The Lowdown Rereading, Revising, and Editing Blues" was written to instill the habits of revision and editing through purposeful rereading aloud. Features covered are rereading for meaning, grammar, syntax, capitalization, punctuation, and spelling. The refrain begins in the voice of the instructor giving commands, is taken over by the student as a necessary chore to be endured, and is finally celebrated in the end as a mission accomplished. The verses elaborate on the editing features. The prompts that the student should be thinking of at each step are outlined below:

Reread	"Read it *out loud*!"	Pair the eyes with the voice to see if you wrote what you wanted, with no omissions or extra words.
Revise	"Does it *sound* right?"	Reread to hear if it makes sense and is written in a way that people really speak (correct grammar and syntax).
Edit	"Does it *look* fine?"	Reread to see if spelling, capital letters, and punctuation are correct.

To rap or sing the song, classes may be split into two groups: one group playing the part of the writer, and the other group playing the part of the teacher and saying the prompts that are in parentheses.

The writing bookmarks are designed for the writer to keep nearby while working. As you introduce the components, students can add a graphic design in the appropriate box that will remind them of what that feature is. This will also show you which features have already been covered to help guide your lesson planning. Once the bookmarks are completed, laminating them will make them last a little longer. Bookmarks can also be used as checklists of items to review after a piece has been written to make sure everything has been covered in the writing.

Each of the features in the songs should ideally be introduced in a separate mini-lesson and then practiced within the writer's workshop. I have included a sample lesson plan to show how you can begin incorporating the songs into your own lessons. As you address each component in a mini-lesson, you can focus on the verses that apply and omit those that don't. The refrain is a summary of the main points, and the verses explain the components with more detail. You may rearrange the order of verses to suit your needs.

In the Resources section you will find selected references by long-established educators with suggestions for lessons and samples of writing for specific features. These songs are meant to be used as reminders during writing as well as acknowledgment of the labor involved in finishing a piece of writing to the satisfaction of the author and an anticipated audience. As with all of the pieces in this book, feel free to rap or sing depending on your comfort level and the wishes of your class.

Writing Form Lesson

Materials

- Chart paper, chalkboard, white board, or SMART Board
- Two nonfiction books with chapters and headings for you to present
- Enough nonfiction books to use in small groups of 2 or 3 students, two books per group
- One index card for you to model
- Two large index cards for each small group to record their book information
- Copy of "My Writing Form Tips" lyrics in large format (overhead, chart paper, etc.)

Large Group Lesson (10 minutes)

"Today we're going to talk about how to start a piece of writing. First I want to show you some books." Show the cover. "What do you think this book is about? How do you know that?" (By the title or picture on the cover.) "Since this book is about horses, tell me what you already know about horses." Write down what they know in list form on the chart paper/board. "Now, what do you think this author will tell us about horses? Let's look at the table of contents." Note the categories listed as chapters or open the book to headings if there is no table of contents. "Let's look at our list of what we know about horses. Would these facts fit into this book? Where?" Discuss. "So the author has chosen one big topic, horses, to write the book about and has decided to write about some other midsized topics about horses to organize the facts. Now let's look at this book." Show another book. "What is the topic or main idea of this book?" Write the topic on the board. "What midsized topics or categories do you think the author would write about in this book?" Write them as bullet points underneath the main topic. Leave large spaces for later lessons in adding details. "Let's look at the categories inside and see if they are the same." You can check off categories that are the same, if you like.

Small Group Practice (15 minutes)

"Now we are going to work in small groups with other books and do the same thing. Each group will work together to find the topic or main idea of the book and then make a short list of the midsized categories underneath, just as we did on the board. You will record your information on the index cards I give you, like this." Write the topic of the second book at the top, then three or four categories in bullet form underneath. "I will give each group two cards and two books to work with." Field any questions and clarify instructions as necessary. Walk around and help groups that need assistance during the small group work.

Large Group Summary (10 minutes)

"Please bring your books and cards back to our large group. Let's share what you found." One student can hold the book up as another student reports the main idea and midsized categories. Spend about 10 minutes hearing from the various groups and talking about the main topic and midsized categories. "Thank you for sharing your books and topics. Now here's a song that talks about what we have done today." Use a large-format chart with verses 2 and 3 covered up. Say the words first, pointing to the chart, then rap or sing the refrain and verse 1, if desired, or have students join in for a second reading with you, rapping the words without a melody.

What's Next? (5 minutes)

"We will continue to work with big topics and midsized categories in our writing workshop. Think of a big topic you would like to write about. Turn to your neighbor and share your idea." After a minute, ask the students to share what their partner said. Then give students a Writing Form bookmark to draw their own big idea in the Introduce section.

My Writing Form Tips

Kathleen Leatherwood

My Writing Form Tips

so that they will stay._____ Un - der your big
brain cells start to dance. Each mid - size cat - e -
in - ner thoughts to tell. By now you're al - most

top - ic choose some oth - ers to ad - dress:_____ Those
go - ry should have de - tails you will show. Us - ing
fin-ished but the end's a vi - tal part. Your con -

mid-size cat - e - gor-ies__ will help you re - duce stress.
all your sen - ses wise-ly ev'-ry read - er then will know.
clu - sion tells the read-er fi - nal thoughts right from your heart.

My Writing Form Tips
Lyrics

IDSEE ("Itsy")

I   **I**ntroduce the topic

D   **D**azzle with detail (word choice)

S   **S**how in detail (senses)

E   **E**xplain in detail (sentence structure)

E   **E**nd with a conclusion

Refrain:

With an "IDSEE" bit of planning
    you can write with much more ease.
Just remember these five points
    and your readers you will please.

Introduce your topic,
    Dazzle words can make it fun.
Show your details and **e**xplain well,
    Then **e**nd it when you're done.

Verse 1:

Start with **I** and **I**ntroduce
    your big **I**dea right away.
Your readers need to know the topic
    so that they will stay.
Under your big topic
    Choose some others to address:
Those mid-size categories
    will help you reduce stress.

Verse 2:

You should choose your words precisely,
    all your readers to entrance.
Reading words that really **D**azzle,
    makes their brain cells start to dance!
Each mid-size category
    should have details you will **S**how.
Using all your senses wisely
    every reader then will know.

Verse 3:

Readers like to know the reasons,
    so **E**xplain your details well.
Please use complex sentence structures,
    your most inner thoughts to tell.
By now you're almost finished,
    but the **E**nd's a vital part.
Your conclusion tells the reader
    final thoughts right from your heart.

My Writing Form Tips
Chords

Refrain: (Use after each verse, or as you like)

                    C   G
With an "IDSEE" bit of planning, you can write with much more ease.
             D7   G   G7
Just remember these five points and your readers you will please.
     C   G
Introduce your topic; dazzle words can make it fun.
                D7   G   C   G
Show your details and explain well, then end it when you're done.

         D7   G
1. Start with **I** and Introduce your big **I**dea right away.
       D7   G
   Your readers need to know the topic, so that they will stay.
   C   G
   Under your big topic choose some others to address:
          D7   G   C   G
   Those midsize categories will help you reduce stress.

         D7   G
2. You should choose your words precisely, all your readers to entrance.
       D7   G
   Reading words that really **D**azzle, makes their brain cells start to dance!
   C   G
   Each midsize category should have details you will **S**how.
   D7   G   C   G
   Using all your **S**enses wisely every reader then will know.

My Writing Form Tips
Chords

                D7   G
3. Readers like to know the reasons, so **E**xplain your details well.
                    D7   G
    Please use complex sentence structures, your most inner thoughts to tell.
          C   G
    By now you're almost finished, but the **E**nd's a vital part.
              D7   G   C   G
    Your conclusion tells the reader final thoughts right from your heart.

Refrain:
                        C   G
    With an "IDSEE" bit of planning you can write with much more ease.
                D7   G   G7
    Just remember these five points, and your readers you will please.
          C   G
    Introduce your topic; dazzle words can make it fun.
                D7   G   C   G
    Show your details and explain well, then end it when you're done.

End

Explain

Show

Dazzle

Introduce

IDSEE

Writing Form Tips

End

Explain

Show

Dazzle

Introduce

IDSEE

Writing Form Tips

End

Explain

Show

Dazzle

Introduce

IDSEE

Writing Form Tips

The Editing Blues Lesson 1

Materials

- Chart paper, chalkboard, white board, or SMART Board
- My lunch story or a similar story of your own where you did not check your writing for accuracy
- A sample draft from another class or one you create to use as a model on SMART Board or overhead. Select a piece that has points that would be resolved by rereading, revising, and editing, using the chorus as a guide. You probably want to select only one or two points from the rap verses to address at a time. You can find writing samples at various levels on the Internet or use your own students' writing.
- A piece of writing from each student in draft form, ready for revising
- Copy of "The Editing Blues" lyrics in large format (overhead, chart paper, etc.)
- "Editing Blues" bookmark for each student

Introduction (5 minutes)

On the chalkboard, white board, or SMART Board, have the following written before the class enters:

Jen Savory   *turkey avocado with chips*

Tell the class that you are going to tell a true story that happened to another teacher that inspired a rap about writing. Here's the story:

Each Friday at the school where Ms. Leatherwood taught, the teachers could order a special lunch to be delivered to school. Everyone looked forward to the special lunch, and one Friday Ms. L went into the office to order hers right before school started. The office was full of teachers, parents, students, and was very loud. Several people wanted to talk to Ms. L, so it was difficult to concentrate on ordering her lunch. Jen Savory showed her the list *(point to board)* and Ms. L noticed that Ms. Savory was getting the turkey avocado sandwich with chips, which was also Ms. L's favorite. So Ms. L wrote down the same thing, while she was also answering another teacher's question *(write on the board, looking frequently over your shoulder, telling the story while writing)*. Then Ms. Savory said, "Write down your name also." So Ms. L, still talking with another teacher, wrote down her name *(write Jen Savory underneath the other Jen Savory)*:

Jen Savory   *turkey avocado with chips*

Jen Savory   *turkey avocado with chips*

(The students will probably notice what happened, but will wait for the end of the story.) So Ms. L went back to her classroom and taught her morning classes, looking forward to her delicious meal. At lunchtime she went to the teacher's lounge and looked for her lunch. There was no container with her name on it. The other teachers said that there were two lunches for Jen Savory, but none with Ms. L's name on it. Ms. L went to the office to see what had happened, and asked to look at the original order. There in front of her, *in her own handwriting* was "Jen Savory, turkey avocado with chips!" *(Point to the board.)* Ms. L went back to the teacher's lounge and discovered that Jen had divided up the lunch among the other teachers, thinking it was an extra, so Ms. L had to go to the school cafeteria and buy *another* meal. After lunch, Ms. L went to her writing workshop class and told them what had happened to her. One student said, "Ms. L, you didn't *reread* what you wrote!" And another student said, "Ms. L, you weren't *listening* to yourself when you were writing!" These were all things Ms. L had told her students to do, and now she realized that she should have done them herself! So Ms. L went home and wrote the rap we are going to learn today.

The Editing Blues Lesson 1

Large Group Lesson (10 minutes)

"Ms. Leatherwood realized there were three things writers should do when they are writing, and a way to check them." Write on the board:

Reread	Read it *out loud*
Revise	Does it *sound* right?
Edit	Does it *look* fine?

"Let's look at this piece of writing." Read the first sentence out loud and ask the students if it *sounds* right. Go through three or four more sentences, reading aloud and revising, making sure that the writing sounds like standard written English. After that, go back to the beginning and see if the words all *look* right (editing). "Here's how Ms. Leatherwood started her song," (show verses 1 and 2 and the first two refrains on an overhead or chart paper). Depending on how much editing the students have already learned, you may want to add one other verse but you don't want to overwhelm them with too much at first. Read through the selected verses and refrains with the students reading aloud with you.

Small Group Practice (15 minutes)

"Now you will be taking your own writing piece and going through these same steps of Rereading, Revising, and Editing to see if your paper is really finished. You will be working in pairs, reading out loud to hear if it sounds right and rereading out loud another time using your eyes to see if everything looks right. It may be easier for you to read your partner's paper instead of reading your own to make sure you are actually reading what was *written*, and not what the writer *meant* to write. Make any changes that would make the paper easier to understand."

Large Group Summary (10 minutes)

"Let's come back to the large group and see what you have noticed when you were rereading your papers." Use the following questions if these points are not brought up naturally when partners are sharing in the large group: Did you make any changes? Did you make changes because they didn't *sound* right or *look* right? Did anyone notice that there were grammatical errors or words left out? Did you think of another way to write something once you reread what you had already written? Did you *think* you had written what you wanted, but you actually wrote something else instead?

What's Next? (5 minutes)

"In the next few weeks we will be learning more verses that will help you revise and edit your writing. Here is a bookmark that will remind you of what to check for in your writing. As we cover the other topics, you may draw in an image that will help you remember it. You may draw an image in the first box, "Read Out Loud," since we covered that topic today. Let's end with rapping the first two verses and refrains again as a whole group." Optional: "Everyone stand up, and let's see if we can add a simple side step and touch while we are reading." Step to R, touch L foot next to R, then step L, touch R foot next to L, like a gospel choir might when singing. You may also add the instrumental or vocal music if you like.

The Lowdown Rereading, Revising, and Editing Blues

Kathleen Leatherwood

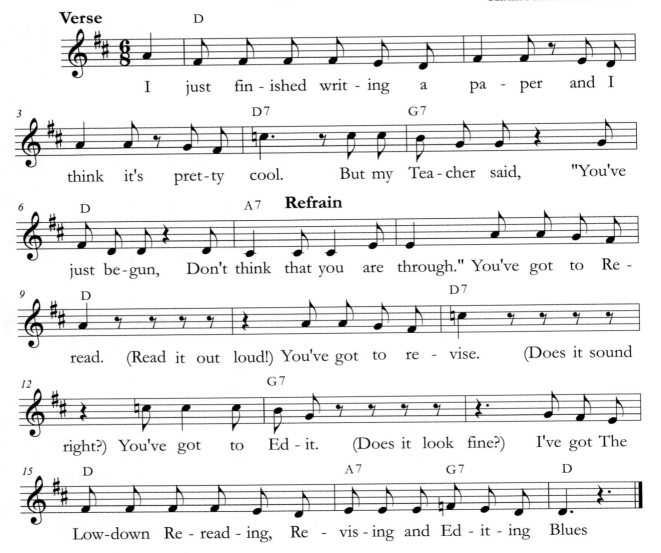

2. I'm reading out loud to hear
If I wrote what I wanted to say.
If I'm not really listening while writing,
My hand just gets carried away.

Refrain 2-5:
I've got to reread ("Read it out loud!")
I've got to revise ("Does it sound right?")
I've got to edit ("Does it look fine?")
I've got the Lowdown Rereading,
Revising, and Editing Blues!

3. I know what it should sound like
With verbs and nouns that match.
So I'll read it out loud to listen again
For those errors I have to catch.

4. Did I start with a capital letter,
When I wrote my sentences down?
Did I use the right punctuation,
So my readers do not frown?

5. Do all the words I used
Look like words I've seen before?
I'll have a go at spelling them right
So my readers don't walk out the door.

6. I've reread my work many times now.
It makes sense and the spelling
looks right.
Punctuation and capital letters
are there,
And the grammar and usage are tight.

CODA: (refrain melody)

I had to reread. (I did it out loud!)
I had to revise. (It all sounds right!)
I had to edit. (It looks great, too!)
I'm **over** The Lowdown Rereading,
Revising, and Editing Blues!

© 2009 Kathleen Leatherwood

146

The Lowdown Rereading, Revising, and Editing Blues
Lyrics

1. I just finished writing a paper
   And I think it's pretty cool.
   But my teacher said, "You've just begun,
   Don't think that you are through."

Refrain Verse 1:

"You've got to reread. (Read it out loud!")
"You've got to revise. (Does it sound right?")
"You've got to edit. (Does it look fine?")
I've got the Lowdown Rereading,
Revising, and Editing Blues!

2. I'm reading out loud to hear
   If I wrote what I wanted to say.
   If I'm not really listening while writing,
   My hand just gets carried away.

Refrain Verses 2-5:

I've got to reread. ("Read it out loud!")
I've got to revise. ("Does it sound right?")
I've got to edit. ("Does it look fine?")
I've got the Lowdown Rereading,
    Revising, and Editing Blues!

3. I know what it should sound like
   With verbs and nouns that match.
   So I'll read it out loud to listen again
   For those errors I have to catch.

4. Did I start with a capital letter
   When I wrote my sentences down?
   Did I use the right punctuation
   So my readers do not frown?

5. Do all the words I used
   Look like words I've seen before?
   I'll have a go at spelling them right
   So my readers don't walk out the door.

6. I've reread my work many times now.
   It makes sense and the spelling looks
       right.
   Punctuation and capital letters are there,
       and the grammar and usage are tight.

CODA: (refrain melody)

I had to reread. (I read it out loud!)
I had to revise. (It all sounds right!)
I had to edit. (It looks great, too!)
I'm **over** The Lowdown Rereading,
    Revising, and Editing Blues!

The Lowdown Rereading, Revising, and Editing Blues
Chords

      D   **D7**
1. I just finished writing a paper and I think it's pretty cool.

              G7   **D**   **A7**

But my teacher said, "You've just begun, don't think that you are through."

Refrain: **(Verse 1 only)**

                               D

"You've got to reread. (Read it out loud!")

                             D7

"You've got to revise. (Does it sound right?")

                        G7

"You've got to edit. (Does it look fine?")

                        D   **A7**   **G7**   **D**

I've got the Lowdown Rereading, Revising, and Editing Blues!

      D   **D7**
2. I'm reading out loud to hear if I wrote what I wanted to say.

              G7   **D**   **A7**

If I'm not really listening while writing, my hand just gets carried away.

Refrain: **(Verses 2-5, use as you like between verses)**

                               D

I've got to reread. ("Read it out loud!")

                             D7

I've got to revise. ("Does it sound right?")

                        G7

"I've got to edit. ("Does it look fine?")

                        D   **A7**   **G7**   **D**

I've got the Lowdown Rereading, Revising, and Editing Blues!

The Lowdown Rereading, Revising, and Editing Blues

Chords

   D   D7

3. I know what it should sound like, with verbs and nouns that match.

    G7   D   A7

  So I'll read it out loud to listen again for those errors I have to catch.

   D   D7

4. Did I start with a capital letter, when I wrote my sentences down?

    G7   D   A7

  Did I use the right punctuation, so my readers do not frown?

   D   D7

5. Do all the words I used look like words I've seen before?

    G7   D   A7

  I'll have a go at spelling them right so my readers don't walk out the door.

   D   D7

6. I've reread my work many times now. It makes sense and the spelling looks right.

    G7   D   A7

  Punctuation and capital letters are there, and the grammar and usage are tight.

CODA: (Refrain melody)

        D

      I had to reread. (I read it out loud!)

        D7

      I had to revise. (It all sounds right!)

        G7

      I had to edit. (It looks great, too!)

          D   A7   G7   D

      I'm <u>over </u>the Lowdown Rereading, Revising, and Editing Blues!

Writing Reminders

Reread		Revise		Edit	
Does it sound right?		Does it look fine?			
Read Out Loud	Grammar & Usage	Capitalization	Punctuation		Have a Go at Spelling

Writing Reminders

Reread		Revise		Edit	
Does it sound right?		Does it look fine?			
Read Out Loud	Grammar & Usage	Capitalization	Punctuation		Have a Go at Spelling

Writing Reminders

Reread		Revise		Edit	
Does it sound right?		Does it look fine?			
Read Out Loud	Grammar & Usage	Capitalization	Punctuation		Have a Go at Spelling

Resources for Teachers

These publications were available as of October, 2012.

Alexander, Rosemary; Susan Gaustad, and Loren Simmons, compilation. 1983. *Poetry Place Anthology,* Instructor Books, (Scholastic Books), New York: Edgell Communications, Inc.

Bear, Donald R., Marcia Invernizzi, Shane Templeton, and Francine Johnston. 1999. *Words Their Way: Word Study for Phonics, Vocabulary, and Spelling Instruction,* second edition, New York: Prentice Hall.

Bintz, William P. "Singing across the Curriculum." *The Reading Teacher,* 63.8 (2010): 683–686.

Calkins, Lucy McCormick. 1986. *The Art of Teaching Writing,* Portsmouth, NH: Heinemann.

Cary, Stephen. 2004. *Going Graphic: Comics at Work in the Multilingual Classroom.* Portsmouth, NH: Heinemann.

Fischer, Phyllis E. 1993. *The Sounds and Spelling Patterns of English,* Farmington, ME: Oxton House Publishers.

Fay, Kathleen, and Suzanne Whaley. 2004. *Becoming One Community: Reading and Writing with English Language Learners,* Portland, ME: Stenhouse Publishers.

Fletcher, Ralph and JoAnn Portalupi. 1998. *Craft Lessons: Teaching Writing K–8,* Portland, ME: Stenhouse Publishers.

Fletcher, Ralph and JoAnn Portalupi. 2001. *Writing Workshop: The Essential Guide,* Portsmouth, NH: Heinemann.

Forney, Melissa. 2001. *Razzle Dazzle Writing: Achieving Excellence through 50 Target Skills.* Gainesville, FL: Maupin House Publishing, Inc.

Fountas, Irene C. and Gay Su Pinnell. 2006. *The Fountas and Pinnell Leveled Book List, K–8,* Portsmouth, NH: Heinemann.

Fountas, Irene C. and Gay Su Pinnell. 2002. *Guided Reading: Good First Teaching for All Children.* Portsmouth, NH: Heinemann.

Fountas, Irene C. and Gay Su Pinnell. 2001. *Guiding Readers and Writers, Grades 3–6: Teaching Comprehension, Genre, and Content Literacy*, Portsmouth, NH: Heinemann.

Fountas, Irene C. and Gay Su Pinnell. 1999. *Matching Books to Readers: Using Leveled Books in Guided Reading, K–3*, Portsmouth, NH: Heinemann.

Freeman, David E., and Yvonne S. Freeman. 2000. *Teaching Reading in Multicultural Classrooms*. Portsmouth, NH: Heinemann.

Freeman, Yvonne S. and David E. Freeman. 2002. *Closing the Achievement Gap: How to Reach Limited-Formal-Schooling and Long-Term English Learners*, Portsmouth, NH: Heinemann.

Fry, Edward B., Jacqueline E. Kress, and Dona Lee Fountoukidis. 2000. *The Reading Teacher's Book of Lists,* fourth edition, Paramus, NJ: Prentice Hall.

Ganske, Kathy. 2000. *Word Journeys: Assessment-Guided Phonics, Spelling, and Vocabulary Instruction*, New York: The Guilford Press.

Graham, Carolyn. 1993. *Grammarchants: More Jazz Chants*, New York: Oxford University Press.

Hannaford, Carla. 1995. *Smart Moves: Why Learning Is Not All in Your Head.* Salt Lake City, UT: Great River Books.

Heard, Georgia. 2002. *The Revision Toolbox: Teaching Techniques That Work*, Portsmouth, NH: Heinemann.

Hill, Jane D., and Kathleen M. Flynn. 2006. *Classroom Instruction That Works with English Language Learners*, Alexandria, VA: Association for Supervision and Curriculum Development.

Holdaway, D. 1979. *Foundations of Literacy.* Sydney: Scholastic.

Kealey, James and Donna Inness. 1997, 2002. *Shananigames: Grammar-Focused Interactive ESL/EFL Activities and Games*, Brattleboro, VT: Pro Lingua Associates, Publishers.

Laminack, Lester L. 2007. *Cracking Open the Author's Craft: Teaching the Art of Writing*, New York: Scholastic, Inc.

McGuinness, Carmen and Geoffrey McGuinness. 1998. *Reading Reflex: The Foolproof Phono-Graphix® Method for Teaching Your Child to Read*, New York: Simon & Schuster.

McGuinness, Carmen and Geoffrey McGuinness. 2000. *How to Increase Your Child's Verbal Intelligence, the Language Wise Method*, New Haven and London: Yale University Press.

McGuinness, Diane. 2004. *Growing a Reader from Birth: Your Child's Path from Language to Literacy*, New York: W. W. Norton & Company, Inc.

Miller, Debbie. 2002. *Reading with Meaning: Teaching Comprehension in the Primary Grades.* Portland, ME: Stenhouse Publishers.

Opitz, Michael F. 2009. *Comprehension and English Language Learners: 25 Oral Reading Strategies That Cross Proficiency Levels.* Portsmouth, NH: Heinemann.

Pinnell, Gay Su, and Patricia L. Scharer. 2003. *Teaching for Comprehension in Reading, Grades K–2.* New York: Scholastic, Inc.

Portalupi, JoAnn, and Ralph Fletcher. 2001. *Nonfiction Craft Lessons: Teaching Information Writing K–8*, Portland, ME: Stenhouse Publishers.

Ray, Katie Wood, with Lester Laminack. 2001. *The Writing Workshop: Working through the Hard Parts (And They're All Hard Parts)*, Urbana, IL: National Council of Teachers of English.

Routman, Regie. 2003. *Reading Essentials: The Specifics You Need to Teach Reading Well*, Portsmouth, NH: Heinemann.

Terban, Marvin. 1993. *Scholastic Guides: Checking Your Grammar*, New York: Scholastic, Inc.

Wolf, Maryanne. 2008. *Proust and the Squid: The Story and Science of the Reading Brain.* New York: Harper Perennial.

Helpful Websites

These websites were active as of October 2012.

www.uiowa.edu/~acadtech/phonetics
An excellent resource with audio and video demonstrating the sounds of the English language (American and British).

www.phono-graphix.com
The website for Phono-Graphix® materials and instruction by Carmen and Geoffrey McGuinness.

www.readamericaclinic.com
The website for the Read America Clinic, owned by Erin Duncan, continuing the clinical work of Carmen and Geoffrey McGuinness.

www.readwritethink.org/parent-afterschool-resources/games-tools/comic-creator-a-30237.html
Comic creator has an interactive program for creating a comic strip with speech and thought balloons, backgrounds, and characters.

http://guest.portaportal.com/contentresources
Resources for second-language learners, but also appropriate for anyone studying English.

http://home.comcast.net/~ngiansante
Lists of leveled books for grades K–6 and older, by title or author and with grade levels and Fountas and Pinnell levels.

http://reading.ecb.org
Reading strategy instruction and practice for students and teachers. Videos of students explaining strategies, lesson plans, and activities.

www.storylineonline.net
Books read aloud by well-known actors.

http://en.childrenslibrary.org
A selection of books from around the world in a variety of languages. Books are not read aloud on the website.

Acknowledgements

Many people have contributed to this collection of raps and songs. My appreciation for their gifts of time and talent is deep, and their acknowledgment here is tiny compared to their impact on the final product. Every comment, suggestion, and insight was considered; many were incorporated.

Good friends and colleagues I have known throughout my life have supported this effort. While teaching English for Speakers of Other Languages (ESOL) at Sunrise Valley Elementary School in Reston, Virginia, the support of principals Chris Brogan and Beth English and their assistant principals Mona Weisman and Carol Burns was always forthcoming. Fairfax County reading teachers Cheryl Freeman, Ava Wolfram, and Carrie Brotemarkle were instrumental in building my knowledge of reading and writing. Social worker Diane Spirer kindly looked over the entire book with me one afternoon and gave her approval of its scope, clarity, and accessibility. Librarian Katie Pieruccini, whose imagination and wit are legend, was kind to listen to my raps from the very beginning and review the final project. Thank you, Jen Savory, who allowed me to explore and utilize a teachable moment during lunch one day and to use her real name in the Writing Blues lesson plan.

Fairfax County ESOL Administrators also had a hand in my developing understanding of how English is acquired and learned. Teddi Predaris, Berthica Rodriguez McCleary, Pat Sheffield, Diane Kerr, Eileen Delaney, Jean Bender, Thea Mallion, Erica Meadows, Kent Buckley-Ess, and Joanne Chen always remained cheerful and helpful despite my frequent questions and requests. These raps and songs are a tribute to their perseverance, spirit, and humor in advocating for English Language Learners of all ages.

While the support of administration is vital, it is the students and teachers on the front lines that provided the motivation for me to create these raps and songs. From 2002 until 2010 my ESOL students and their peers kept me on my toes as they challenged me to help them navigate the English language. Their need for clear, succinct practice to help them speak, read, write, and understand what they heard led to these materials. The number of students is too large to list by name here, but they will know themselves from the years mentioned and have my heartfelt thanks for inspiring me. I would also like to acknowledge Rebecca Grundahl and her parents, Tina Thinglev and Henrik Grundahl, who allowed me to tell her story and gave permission to use her artwork in this book.

As for the teachers I have known and worked with, I remain grateful and awestruck by their talent, generosity, and dedication to learning. Teachers from schools in Germany, Argentina, Africa, Minnesota, Maryland, and Virginia listened to these raps/songs and gave valuable feedback. Cheryl Allen shared her classrooms with me; her writing, compassion and teaching craft are great. Darlene Doley, master teacher, inspired me with her dry wit and insight. Kathy Lamkin, friend and co-teacher, helped me keep the style consistent and logical within the vowel songs. Margot Neurohr, my roommate at Sunrise Valley, deserves thanks for her boundless enthusiasm, support, and verve. Linda Blake's high aspirations for her students, and her willingness to let me try my ideas, helped forge a lifelong friendship. Tam Frishberg gave me a strong grounding in teaching reading while in Germany and helped me clarify the Reading Strategies song. Ioulia Liebermann helped me clarify the Editing Blues with her perspective of having learned English as a second language. Amelia Arraya, an English teacher in Argentina, kept up with the growing number of songs over the years and offered feedback. Phono-Graphix teachers Jenny Taylor of Read for Africa and Safiyan Fareed in South Carolina were enthusiastic as I showed them the correlation of the songs to the code of English.

Another set of teachers were brave enough to test drive these raps and songs in their classrooms throughout the years. Katie Booth and I co-taught Word Study together in her third grade classroom. Ji

Ahn opened her classroom for me to teach her fifth and sixth grade students both writing songs and offered valuable feedback on the cover art. Kris Barna volunteered her class for me to lead a lesson on questioning strategies, field-testing the "Reading Strategies Lesson—Intermediate" song and bookmark. Eben Montaquila's fifth grade class also tried out the song. Marty Van OpDorp at South Lakes High School generously mentored me, shared his students, and led me on numerous adventures in the name of cutting edge learning techniques and performance art. First grade teachers Anisha Goveas-Foti and Carrie Holland are generously trying out some of the songs in their first grade classrooms as this book goes to print. Concurrently, Mary Jackson has taken some grammar raps to Rwanda for use with the Urukundo Preschoolers to supplement what Arlene Brown took back to her kids in 2010. I am grateful to all of them for their frankness, encouragement, and trust.

In addition to the above, I also called upon some outstanding teachers from years past who had faith in me. Department of Defense Dependents Schools teachers Jan Johnson, Cindi and Rick Ervin, Kathy and Dan Morrow, and Jim and Shery Hancock believed in my creativity so many years ago. There is a great deal of their love of children, music, and humor in these songs. Rick and Cindi not only gave comments but also passed the songs along to their former elementary principal, Shawne Cryderman, whose advice will ensure that the music CD includes a vocal as well as an instrumental track for each song. I turned to Gloria Michau, a Fairfax County reading teacher for twenty-four years, to confirm the songs' clarity and usefulness. Mic Weinblatt, art teacher, playwright, and drama director, with whom I worked on musical productions, took time to look over my work and share his enthusiasm. Pam Olmes along with Joanne Bury, a former ESOL teacher for high school and adults, looked over the songs for relevance with older students. Looking out for our youngest learners, Sheila Doyle, Linda Blake, and Lorene Lacava considered the Grammar Raps for use in preschool and kindergarten classrooms. Thank you to poet Oni Lasana for her wisdom and friendship and for showing me that there is poetry in all of us.

While writing the songs in this book I was eager to receive feedback from musicians, and am thankful for their contributions. Music teachers Jack Layne and Jennifer Frazier helped tweak the keys and rhythms so that what was printed matched my concept and worked with a variety of voices. Musicians Sy Zucker and Jerry and Petie Hebenstreit looked at the music for originality and musicality to ensure that it was not derivative of existing songs. My son Ben assembled our in-home studio and patiently guided me in creating the rap rhythms and music files for the practice CD.

My editorial reviewers have my utmost gratitude for their eagle eyes and facility with the English language. Bill Doyle, my former boss in Germany and a stellar writer, took on the task of looking over the introduction. His suggestions, as always, were spot on. Cheryl Freeman not only observed my teaching in Ji Ahn's classroom and offered feedback but also suggested revisions for the book's introduction. Faith Leonard deserves credit for suggesting the clear descriptors on the chord and lyric pages as well as in the introduction. Joy Onozuka, professional editor and translator, made suggestions about publishing and marketing. In spite of the considerable help in editing, I alone am responsible for any mistakes that may still exist.

In order to get my songs on paper and to publication, it was necessary to find the right software. Isaac S. and Jesse G. at MakeMusic Customer Support found solutions to my queries regarding the Finale PrintMusic software with which these songs were written. Friend Katie McCall guided me through the mysteries of PDF files. I credit them all for helping give the songs a clean, professional look.

Many thanks are also in order to the folks at SelfPublishing.com, who gave me the guidance necessary to self-publish this book. Kathy Rodgers and Jonathan Gullery were on board in the very beginning, answering questions about publishing music. My coach, Phil Whitmarsh, has been a saint in fielding my constant requests for clarification on publishing points. I thank Carolyn Madison and the editorial department at Self Publishing, Inc. for their expertise and diligence. This book would look a lot different had these folks not had a hand in its final product.

Although they are mentioned within the book, I would be remiss if I did not again acknowledge Carmen and Geoffrey McGuinness and Carolyn Graham. These songs came about because of my belief in the Phono-Graphix paradigm created by the McGuinnesses. They have my highest respect for their elegant, straightforward principles of the English language. The grammar raps were inspired by Carolyn Graham's workshop at the 2003 TESOL convention in Baltimore and gave me a vehicle for my students to learn spoken English. Graham's energy and sense of humor set the tone for my own work, and I am thankful for her paving the way.

Having mentioned so many people who have been a part of this endeavor, this book would not exist without the support of my friends and family. For years of friendship and encouragement, I thank Lynda and Al Parrella, Joyce and Henry Hebert, Charles and Phyllis Wynn, Linda and Zach Hubbard, Julie Berla, and Michelle Crnkovich. You have been a constant treasure to me. Chris Parrott and Christina Viscomi, fellow ESOL teachers, listened to these songs as they were written. Tim Stanley, newly retired principal, admired the simplicity of the materials despite the complexity of the subject. My gratitude goes to colleague and friend Mariella Walker, who acted as my substitute teacher when necessary, took over my position when I left Sunrise Valley, and believed in this project from the beginning. I believe Cheryl Holm, no longer on this earth, is somewhere looking down and winking.

My book group, Melanie Stanley, Becky Anzelone, Beth Heiman, and Marie Wright, keep me sane and jolly as we discuss books over copious amounts of food, drink, and laughter. Lyn Loy, my amazing physical therapist, has been unwavering in her support for this project, keeping not only my spirits in good shape but my muscles and joints. Dear friend and prolific artist, Martha Kopp Bless, suggested that visuals would add to the songs. Martha, Melanie, Becky, and Lyn coached me in drawing the faces you see on the student pages. When the time came for the cover, I was excited that Becky agreed to help, adding her experience in both art and computer graphics. Melanie graciously agreed to take the photo for the back cover. All these women have been so amazingly steadfast in their friendship and support of this book, that words cannot describe how grateful I am. You are truly my soul sisters.

My family has given me the confidence and time to devote to these raps and songs. My husband, David, son, Ben, and his girlfriend, Schuyler, have read over possibly every part of this book at some point in time and *still* cheer me on. The Leatherwood side of the family: Sue, Bud, Greg, Steve, Diana, Suzie, and their families have also been stalwart supporters of these songs. My mom, Louisa Walker, who bravely stepped in when our mother passed away, has always been there for me. My siblings Barb, John, Melissa, and Joe and their families continue to encourage my visits in spite of my inflicting these songs on their offspring. And here's to you, Uncle Frank, for your humor and song; to Aunt Vonne, who also writes books; and to Aunt Helen, who financed this publication from a faraway star. Were they still alive, I feel certain my parents, Brad and Dorothy Walker, would be smiling.

My hearty thanks go to you, the reader, who have selected this book. May you find joy and learning within its pages.

Finally, I would like to thank Pete Seeger, who taught us not only that music can carry a powerful message but also that magic can happen when people gather and sing together. When it comes to understanding the idiosyncrasies of that crazy English language, a little magic couldn't hurt, and may perhaps even help.

Notes